This book is dedicated to my wonderful parents and family in Libya, my amazing wife and in-laws, and my three lovely daughters, also to all those working hard to help ease the suffering of others, but most importantly to my heroes, the frontline citizens who are struggling daily trying to serve and heal my beloved country of Libya.

A JOURNEY of HOPE & HEALING

© 2016, Omar Reda / **Family Bonding Project**
All rights reserved.

No part of this book may be used or reproduced by any means, graphic, electronic, or mechanical, including photocopying, recording, taping or by any information storage retrieval system without the written permission of the author /publisher except in the case of brief quotations embodied in critical articles and reviews.

ISBN: 978-0-9970008-9-4

BOOK DESIGN
timmyroland.com

COVER IMAGE
Sebastian Unrau

English Version

A JOURNEY of **HOPE & HEALING**

OMAR REDA, MD

Family Bonding Project
WORLDWIDE

Liberated
A JOURNEY *of* **HOPE & HEALING**

Contents

About The Author . . . . *i*
Acknowlegements . . . . *iii*
Introduction . . . . *v*
Preface . . . . *vii*
The Spark 1
First Trip 5
Second Trip 9
Third Trip 21
Fouth Trip 37
To Forgive Does Not Mean To Forget 41
Children & War 47
Challenges 51
Now What? 55
The Wounded Healer 59
Academic Detachment 61
Conclusion 63
References 65

Liberated
A JOURNEY of HOPE & HEALING

About the Author

Dr. Omar Reda is a board-certified psychiatrist who currently lives with his wife and three daughters in Portland, Oregon.

He graduated from Benghazi Medical School, obtained a Masters certificate in global mental health from Harvard Program in Refugee Trauma, and then finished psychiatric residency at the University of Tennessee.

Dr. Reda chairs the USA section of the Federation for Arab Psychiatrists, the Oregon Muslim Medical Association and heads the Family Bonding Project. He is also actively involved in multiple youth and family healing and empowerment projects nationally and internationally.

Dr. Reda is an expert and a sought-after public speaker on issues of psychological trauma, Muslims' mental health, immigrants' mental health, the Libyan revolution and the Arab Spring.

Liberated

A JOURNEY of HOPE & HEALING

Acknowledgement

Amanda Lubit, DVM, MPH. Recommendations for Peace-Building and Reconciliation after Ethnic Conflict in the Republic of Kosovo. Portland State University, Portland, Oregon.

Liberated

A JOURNEY of HOPE & HEALING

Introduction

This writing is a modest attempt at evaluating the psychosocial impact of trauma on the psyche of its survivor, using the example of the 2011 Libyan Revolution and subsequent war.

The message I am trying to preach is one of hope. Despite all the suffering the trauma survivors endure, the goal is for them to emerge from that experience with the strong belief in the importance of healing, recovery, rehabilitation and reconciliation.

Resentment and anger only breed continued hostility, violence and bloodshed. It is only through forgiveness and reconciliation that we can ensure peace for our future generations, as well as their physical, emotional, and spiritual health and wellbeing.

I hope that those who are touched and affected by the ugly fires of trauma and violence could become examples to others that one can face dire hardship and extreme evil, yet still heal and thrive.

I invite you to get liberated, and join on this journey of hope and healing.

Liberated
A JOURNEY of HOPE & HEALING

Preface

The praise belongs to Allah who helped me finish memoir that aims at getting the reader unstuck and liberated.

I am currently working on multiple family and youth healing initiatives using my personal experience and professional expertise as an example of how individuals can find hope in the middle of suffering, find meaning, forgiveness and closure in a confusing trauma story and try to preach and live a life of peace.

Let me briefly share some aspects of my trauma story, especially around the 2011 Libyan revolution and subsequent war.

Liberated
A JOURNEY *of* HOPE & HEALING

The Spark

Looking back to December of 2010, I remember my wife standing in front of our sliding glass door, staring aimlessly at a fountain in the backyard. She had a blank look on her face but I could tell that she was deep in thought. I called her name several times before she broke out of her trance. When I asked her what she was staring at, she replied calmly but with trepidation in her voice, "I don't know, I just feel like our lives are about to change forever, I don't know how but I can't shake this feeling." I told her to keep positive thoughts and we didn't talk much more about it until a few days later when I realized how prophetic her words were. The news of a young man setting himself on fire in protest of poor treatment from police in Tunisia dominated the air waves and captivated the world. Whether an act of courage, desperation or both, it ignited a revolution in Tunisia that spread throughout the Arab world, eventually knocking on the front door of my home country, Libya.

The stories, images and videos were uploaded to the internet at an alarming rate, but were they real or

LIBERATED

were they rumors intended to scare the people into submission or rally them against a tyrant. My wife and I were glued to the TV and media outlets looking for any information that may give us hope. The fighting in Benghazi and neighboring cities was becoming more and more intense. We could no longer function, but instead became zombies not able to do anything but stare at a screen. Our children had to grow up overnight and learn to take care of themselves. We provided the basic essentials but could do no more.

I could not focus at work, and my wife did not have the strength or the will to even dress the girls and take them to school. We would make our eighteen-month old daughter a bottle and let her play. They took care of each other as if they too knew what was going on. Although we tried to shelter them, they just knew, they could feel it.

My wife and I had not slept for days; the stress was clearly taking its toll on both of us.

I picked up the phone, hoping, praying to hear the double ring tone that usually meant the call had gone through. Then it happened, I nearly had given up when I finally got through to my mother after days of anticipation and anxiety, she told me that Gaddafi had promised to bomb Benghazi that night by air and sea, that she loved me and was proud of me, that she wanted me to forgive her and that we would meet again in Heaven. The sound of her voice is something I will never forget for the rest of my life. The fact that she, and the rest of my family truly believed that their lives were over, is something that no child should ever hear their mother say. Till this day I can hear her very words in my nightmares. I could no longer contain my emotions; the tears flew from my eyes relentlessly. My wife took the phone and I could remember her saying, "protect yourselves, fight for your lives, cover your windows and get under beds and tables."

We told them all that we loved them and that they had to do whatever it took to survive and that we would do whatever we could to help. As my wife continued to talk to my mother, I came to the conclusion that I had to do something; I had to go to Libya.

Liberated
A JOURNEY of HOPE & HEALING

First Trip

As the world watched in disbelief the atrocities committed, and the human rights violations and crimes against humanity systemically performed before its very eyes, the voice of human consciousness and reason demanded a stop to this non-sense and madness. My wife and I tried frantically to contact human rights organizations, media and international non-governmental organizations; many sympathized with the situation and indicated that they were watching the news very closely, but who knows how many lives would be lost and how many cities would be wiped out before watching would turn into action.

After the phone call with my mother, I knew that I had to fly to Libya, my wife and girls were scared, I asked if any of the NGOs was sending a team, I was blessed to receive a reply from Medical Teams International, an NGO in my very backyard in Portland, Oregon, they expressed their grave concern about the medical needs in Libya, they promised to gather nearly half a million-dollar worth of medications to ship to Libya if I was willing to accompany it, I told them "you bet I was".

LIBERATED

The minute I crossed the Egyptian border to the empty Libyan security checkpoint I had a flood of mixed emotions, the air felt lighter and smelled fresher, I could not stop crying touching my face on the Libyan soil, a dream in the making was about to become a reality, Libya is becoming a land of freedom and dignity.

I entered home unannounced, my mother, sisters and nieces were hysterical, and my nephew who I left fifteen-month old was now in the ninth grade. Beautiful times and precious memories were stolen from me, but now it was time to cherish and enjoy every moment.

I visited many hospitals in Benghazi and towns in the East, as the West and South were still under the control of Gaddafi; I sat with medical and clinical staff that had to deal with images and injuries they never dreamt of encountering. Textbooks did not prepare these young people for such gruesome and graphic images and fatalities, but as they tried to hide their emotions and feelings of distress, anger and fear from their patients they were willing to share them with a caring colleague. Many held back their tears while others generously shared them with their stories. These young men and women were relieved to be given permission to express their feelings, to know that it was okay to be human and that they were not alone.

Given the large body of evidence and research on resilience, especially in the context of an ongoing armed conflict, psychological needs had to wait as medical and surgical wounds took precedence. I insisted however on including mental health in all health cluster meetings and discussions, and made it very clear that I am available and will visit this issue again and again.

The whole country was grieving, as the numbers of the deceased, kidnapped, missing, raped, tortured and injured climbed to the thousands. I knew then that the weeks and months to come will need for me to either travel more frequently or permanently relocate to Libya. Libya needed me and I cannot say no, not now.

The best that my poor wife was able to get from me was the promise that I will not travel to the frontlines unless absolutely necessary and that I will not fight or carry a weapon unless in self-defense, I was lucky to be able to keep both promises despite the temptation.

I was privileged to go back to serve, so I thought that the best use of my time was to do psycho-education and raise awareness about the mental health impact of war through lectures, workshops and media appearances. I was also honored to meet great people in local civil society organizations who were doing wonderful work with survivors.

Liberated
A JOURNEY *of* **HOPE & HEALING**

Second Trip

I reached out to Libyan doctors in the west who were as enthusiastic and caring as I was but who lacked coordination, organization and funding. I was blessed once again to be connected to another organization, Mercy Corps; who was approved to do psychosocial programs with the children in Misrata.

My poor wife almost had a heart attack when she heard the name, Misrata was the scene of some of the most ugly and fierce fights, the city was almost totally destroyed and stories of snipers, mercenaries, mass killing and rape were so fresh in her mind, but God bless her, she too cared about the Libyan children that she made the very difficult decision to allow me to go again.

I was very blessed to have a wonderful and understanding wife, and also supportive colleagues who gave me time off and covered my duties to allow me to go on this mission, they told me that I needed to follow my heart, I am glad that I did because somewhere along that journey I found myself and my true calling.

LIBERATED

My favorite part of the whole mission was the nights of Ramadan. We built a tent in the freedom square in downtown Misrata and started psychosocial activities for children. We had a great success, and parents requested that we expand our programs to other age groups and extend them to other neighborhoods. It was the most fulfilling experience in my entire life. I always loved children but could not specialize as a child psychiatrist because I did not like to see children suffer, but in Misrata I did really enjoy my time and felt that I was making a difference.

The local NGOs were incredibly amazing, their staff and children-friendly activities made a huge difference for kids who lost their parents and struggled to believe that the world could again be a safe and trusted place to live in. I conducted many play and art therapy projects, and these young beautiful girls and boys taught me a lot and helped me become a better physician and human.

We counseled parents and caregivers on ways to deal with issues faced by their children. Some of the common problems we encountered in Libya were nightmares, stuttering, bedwetting, anger at home and poor school performance. Through education and encouraging non-violent ways of dealing with children and through family activities, many of these issues got resolved.

A JOURNEY *of* HOPE & HEALING

One night, a group of fighters came to the tent and told me that it was a shame that I was a fighting age and was not in the frontlines but instead "playing with children", I told them that the tent was indeed my frontline and that I rather use my expertise to help their children cope and heal. Libya deserves that we die for her sake, but deserves also that we live for her sake and help her heal and recover.

We noticed lots of improvement in the writings and drawings of children with psychosocial support and psycho-education. Over the weeks, they stopped drawing blood, tanks and body pieces, and started talking about their schools and friends. Their outlook was focused now on the future rather than on darkness, death and destruction.

Post-Traumatic Stress Disorder (PTSD) is a common phenomenon after a traumatic event, which can lead to either the re-experience of trauma through flashbacks and nightmares, the avoidance of reminders of the trauma, or experiencing physical symptoms like shortness of breath, sweating, hand tremors and palpitations. In the case of children they can have psychosomatic, behavioral and academic struggles.

In Tripoli, I also started activities of my project Libya Al-Shefa with wonderful local NGOs, these activities included psycho-education, support circles for children, women, fighters and families of the

LIBERATED

deceased, on both sides of the conflict.

Here is what my wife Nura wrote while I was in Libya. Every time I read her letter I still cannot hold back my tears, my justification was that my small family in America was safe and comfortable, and that the Libyan children needed a small sacrifice of my time and service.

(When he told me that he needed to go back I didn't know what to do or how to feel. "Why is this happening to me?" is all I kept repeating in my head. The first time Omar went to Libya it was a week into the fighting. "I have to help" is all he kept saying to me. Those days were the worst. Hearing loved ones on the phone telling you that hopefully they would see you in paradise, seeing your husband cry because all he could do was imagine his whole family being killed at the hands of one of the most ruthless dictators in the history of the world was not easy. I had family also in Libya but it wasn't the same. For me, I felt pain for them but my relationship wasn't the same. Omar had his parents and siblings in Libya who he grew up with, I hardly knew my family.

I cried every day, worried about the country I had loved for so long but never able to see or step foot in. The images are ones that etched in my brain and heart forever. Seeing another human being blown to pieces is something no person should ever have to see. The sad thing is that after a while, it became a normal event, just one more person fighting for freedom, or standing in the wrong place at the wrong time.

I begged Omar not to go, I cried and threatened him with everything I had, even though I never meant it. I went as far as telling our three little girls that daddy was leaving us to go to a war zone. That was a huge mistake but I was desperate, he was desperate, what was I supposed to do?

He booked his flight for the next day. He begged for my blessing which I gave with a heavy heart.

That night we held each other tightly crying together, not knowing if we would ever see each other again, if I would be a single mother caring for three little girls who viewed their father as a super Man. I soaked my pillow with tears as he tried to comfort me but his tears were just as heavy. I was so mad at him, so angry but had to let him go, I had to let him do this or he would never forgive himself, and perhaps never forgive me.

My family was surprised and angry Omar was going but they knew that nothing would stop him. The phone call was not an easy one to make. I was not going to be alone during this. I could not risk it. I booked a flight for my daughters and myself to go stay with my family in Colorado while Omar was gone. I laugh now thinking about how angry I was that, because of Omar's lack of planning, I would be booking last minute tickets that cost a fortune. I remember yelling at him about the price of the tickets then feeling terrible about it later.

I just wanted him to stay home. He looked at me like he always does with a calm face and said, "It is fine, everything will be okay." I wanted to believe him but I just couldn't this time, this was real, it was the biggest event to hit both of our lives and one way or another, we both knew that our lives would never be the same.

I pulled the girls out of school early to catch our flight. I got yelled at by the school president for parking in the handicap parking spot. I wanted to stop and explain, I'm not the kind of person who breaks the rules, but I had more important things on my mind. The girls were confused but excited once they found out we were going to grandma and grandpa's house. It dawned on me then that most people would be worried about their kids missing a month of school, will they flunk? will they fail? I didn't care. I needed them to be surrounded by love. I had to be sure that if, God forbids, something happened to Omar, we were not alone.

We said our goodbyes at the airport. I didn't want to let him go. He called my cell phone and left me a message that I still have saved until this day. I would listen to it every night before going to sleep. The nightmares were never ending. I screamed and cried in my sleep for the first time in my life. My mother would tell me every morning. Was I losing it?

For the first time in my life I could honestly say that I know what it feels like to be an army wife except my husband was not in the military. He was entering a war zone, dangerous, unpredictable and growing more violent by the day. He promised that he would come home. I worried, he would stay. His argument to go was that he needed to help. He is a doctor, a psychiatrist with emergency and trauma training. He would be a great asset and a big help.

He worked with Medical Teams International and took half a million dollars of donated medical supplies with him to Libya. "We will be helping so many people!" is all he kept telling me. "I know" was all I could say.

Waiting for his call from Egypt was nerve wracking. I had been waiting for him to call but he missed our agreed upon appointment. We rented a satellite phone that did not work! Another added stress, my only lifeline to Omar was useless. I left my cell phone under my pillow staring at the ceiling with bloodshot burning eyes. I was tired but couldn't sleep. I was hungry but couldn't eat. All I wanted was to hear his voice. Finally, 3:00 in the morning it rang, I heard his voice, we said, "I love you". I cried all night.

LIBERATED

I didn't hear from him again for a few days and then finally a call. He got the phone to work. He was on top of the tallest building in Benghazi. He was excited to get the phone working . . . I was begging him to get down to a safer place. He was happy, happier than I had heard him for a long time. He said he could smell freedom and that the conflict would be over soon. How wrong he was, neither of us knew. Gaddafi was promising to bomb Benghazi, and the snipers were still everywhere.

I called his father and begged him to get Omar out of Libya. He promised he would and kept his word. Three weeks after Omar left, he was home but he came home a different man. His body was here but his mind and heart were in Libya. The images would stay with him forever. He helped as much as he could, in and out of the hospitals tending to the wounded both physically and mentally. He told me that he slept with a machete under his pillow. I don't know what good that would have done had Gaddafi's army made it into their home but what was he supposed to do? He started to talk in his sleep for the first time, and some nights he wakes up shivering in cold sweat. He left to the other room afraid that he might wake me or the baby, not knowing that I was always awake afraid that he might need me. My husband who left to Libya is not the same person who came back, he now carries the pain and suffering of millions on his shoulders, he feels guilty, hardly eats, sleeps, talks or smiles. He is always on the TV and internet looking for good news. The war that started in Libya is still going on in his mind and heart. He was hurt and wounded but did not want to bother anyone with his pain. He wanted to go back to Misrata during the heavy fighting there, this time I did not cry, instead I prayed and asked Allah for help, that Omar gets peace of mind and closure and come back safe. Six months I spent in hell, but trusting Allah I always saw a light at the end of the tunnel. I was always hopeful but treated every moment we had together as it was our last. What was I supposed to do? What was he supposed to do?).

I was able to use my skills in psycho-education, training of trainers, capacity-building with local NGOs and institutions like the schools and orphanages, in addition to filling gaps in clinical services and triage and referral mechanisms with the hope of making a long-lasting impact in Libya through both short-term and long-term efforts, activities, projects and plans.

I was lucky to have a specialized training in mental health during disasters and knew about psychosocial support for war survivors. In addition to my psychiatry residency training, God blessed me to attend a Masters Certificate course through Harvard Program in Refugee Trauma (HPRT) in 2007. I have never thought that I would be using the skills I learnt

LIBERATED

pursuing my passion in trauma mental health in my home country, with my very people, family, relatives, neighbors, friends and colleagues.

How I spent my time in Libya was briefly to divide the day into three periods, mornings between hospitals, clinics and schools, afternoons between local NGOs and lectures, while evenings were dedicated to psychosocial child-friendly activities.

It was amazing to attend the opening ceremonies of local NGOs dedicated to serve children, orphans, families of the deceased and people with special needs. To see Libyans excited to create their own institutions and write their missions, visions and bylaws was just exhilarating.

It was a very difficult decision to leave Libya as I am going through survivor's guilt and have mixed feelings about the need to come back to the USA and care for my small family, get back to a semi-normal routine, go to work, and help the Libyan cause from a distance by fundraising and increasing awareness, and between the desire to go back to Libya and even stay there to help care for the needy and rebuild my home country.

My mission to Libya was again overwhelming and heartbreaking. The people were cautiously optimistic but quite resilient, they needed continued support. Their only request was the same that the young lady from Tripoli made to Anderson Cooper "If I die, I do not want the country or the revolution to die, if I die, I want the whole world to know that I tried to live dignified, if I die, I do not want my death to go in vain"

Libyans are very decent people who deserve the same rights all of us take for granted. These times made me appreciate freedom and people who struggle for their rights. The basic right to live, to feel safe, to have dignity and voice an opinion is basically priceless.

Gaddafi was killed on 10/20/2011, was that closure? was that justice for the families of the dead? will Libya ever recover from this long nightmare? only time can tell.

Liberated
A JOURNEY of HOPE & HEALING

Third Trip

I flew to Libya again in December of 2011 to work on my national reconciliation and healing project. For reconciliation in Libya to be successful, certain prerequisites need to be in place:

1. Legislative reform and political support. The project activities would have to be approved and sanctioned by a bill passed and supported by the Libyan government.

2. Transformative and restorative justice. Healing starts through the transformation of harm by integrating the traumatic experience into the wholeness of its survivor. Emphasis is on repairing damage caused by criminal behavior achieved through cooperative processes that include all stakeholders. The fundamental principles are that justice requires that professionals work to help those who have been injured, and that those most directly involved and affected should have the opportunity to participate fully in the response and recovery programs. The role of government would

be to preserve a just public order as well as secure and safe social and political spaces, while the role of the community would be to nurture and maintain a healing environment.

3. Civil society engagement. A successful reconciliation and healing process requires meaningful engagement of civil society organizations and the public at large.

4. Consensus building. Taking culture into consideration, professionals need to follow the standard guidelines in the field.

5. Truth-telling. To set the record straight and create an environment where forgiveness may occur, the first step is to admit that injustice was committed.

6. Education. There is a need to educate the general public about the experiences of trauma and grief as well as their extent and effect on survivors. There is also a need for education on how communities that have experienced violent conflicts can coexist in peace and harmony.

7. Counseling for trauma and grief. Both through individual and group approaches.

8. Special healing places and community intervention programs. The HOPE project in the freedom square of Misrata is an initiative that could be replicated throughout the country.

9. Memories and rituals need to be celebrated.

10. Funding. One factor that often hinders the progress and success of any long-term project is funding. Reconciliation exercises are not only expensive, but time-consuming emotional ventures that demand patience and resilience.

After more than five decades under Gaddafi's rule and a violent revolution to remove him from power, Libyan society remains severely divided. Since the end of the armed conflict in October 2011, external peacekeeping forces have proposed many methods for preventing further violence; yet, in order to achieve sustainable solutions to these conflicts, a multidisciplinary and collaborative approach must be implemented to ensure local community needs are met.

Reconciliation between conflicting political entities and identities within Libya can only succeed if Libyans themselves feel both invested and involved in these efforts.

LIBERATED

History has shown that traditional, one-sided peace initiatives that focus solely upon rebuilding and strengthening the state structure have proven largely unsuccessful in achieving a lasting peace.

The failure of the international community to localize, contextualize, and build on local understandings of past experiences and existing cultural norms has hindered reconstruction. It has led to the neglect of local participatory structures, the introduction of inappropriate civil society mechanisms, and the creation of new sources of tension, rivalries, and sites of conflict.

While it is necessary to restore state infrastructure following violent conflict, this cannot be the sole focus of peace-building. These types of interventions neglect the needs of individuals and of local communities, both of which must also be addressed in order for society to successfully make the transition to a sustainable peace. For this reason, peace-building and reconciliation programs should implement initiatives that focus upon helping both individuals and communities to emotionally heal from the traumas experienced during armed conflicts.

To address these emotional needs, peace-building initiatives should seek to provide culturally-appropriate psychosocial services for individuals, methods of rebuilding interpersonal connections within communities, and techniques for reopening a dialogue between divided communities. Although post-conflict healing and reconciliation will not occur quickly, these efforts will prove worthwhile because of the sustainable results they can achieve.

When addressing post-conflict situations, peace-building initiatives must adopt a comprehensive approach. For this reason, it is recommended that a combination of collaborative, multidisciplinary, and praxis approaches be utilized to develop peace-building and reconciliation programs. This theoretical approach will allow for engagement with highly controversial issues in both an ethical and comprehensive manner. As a result, this framework has the potential to promote long-term reconciliation projects that will have the support of affected Libyan communities.

Collaboration, the first of these theoretical approaches, involves the inclusion of community members into all stages of program planning, development and implementation. This ensures that indigenous perspectives and needs are incorporated and addressed throughout the process. By encouraging the inclusion of local voices and experiences, this approach allows local participants to shape program development. As a result, these initiatives provide communities with culturally-appropriate and locally relevant methods for resolving conflict and implementing peace.

Additionally, a multidisciplinary approach should also be incorporated into this collaborative framework. The complex and diverse issues associated with violent conflicts require a diverse response by multiple disciplines, ensuring that peace-building projects are as effective and sustainable as possible. The resulting partnership of various experts with community members will ensure that post-conflict tensions are addressed using multiple techniques that apply to a diverse population of affected individuals and communities.

Finally, a praxis theory of practice integrates the collaborative and multidisciplinary theoretical frameworks to create a dynamic approach that further increases the likelihood of attaining sustainable results. Based upon the desire to resolve a specific social issue such as post-conflict tension, the praxis approach promotes the ongoing development of new techniques and theories in order to maximize effectiveness. This means that every time programs address post-conflict tensions, participants can learn from these experiences and gain further knowledge to modify and improve future programs. Consequently, the knowledge and experiences of various collaborators in these programs will continually inform how the project develops over time. These processes of ongoing interaction and feedback will not only assist the continual advancement of these reconciliation programs, but they will also ensure these projects meet the moral responsibilities due to the target communities in Libya.

In 1969, Gaddafi seized control of Libya through a military coup that introduced a dictatorship that would last until 2011. For more than four decades, Gaddafi ruled Libya largely on the basis of tribal affiliation, deepening existing regional and tribal divisions that date back to Ottoman rule (from the 16th to 20th centuries) and the Italian colonization (20th century).

To maintain the absolute power he claimed, Gaddafi outlawed political parties, civil society, media, trade and private ownership. This lack of state infrastructure denied the Libyan people access to many basic necessities and forced them to rely heavily upon traditional kin and tribe networks for support. This decentralizing of the Libyan state resulted in a lack of cohesion between tribes and regions that now poses a challenge for Libya as it seeks to rebuild.

Without a constitution, political parties, elections, active or effective government organizations, officials, or civil servants, Libya lacks a basic governance framework on which to rebuild, and must instead construct an entire state system mostly from scratch. These divisions remain a legacy of the nation's history and of Gaddafi's political practices.

Peace-building and reconciliation initiatives must consider these realities and the challenges they pose when developing future programs for post-conflict Libya.

Lessons learned from other post-conflict interventions can help to inform future efforts taken on behalf of the Libyan people. In the aftermath of other armed conflicts, peacekeeping initiatives have largely failed to create an environment supportive of a sustainable peace. These failures can partially be explained by the habit of many international organizations to make decisions without local involvement, resulting in the neglect of local community needs. In addition, these interventions often fail to use culturally-appropriate methods, alienating the communities they seek to engage who view these programs as foreign and suspicious. As a result, local communities become isolated from these peace-building efforts, preventing these programs from achieving a sustainable peace. These limitations of past reconciliation efforts demonstrate how vital it is for local community members to become actively involved in the processes of reconciliation and peace-building following armed conflicts.

Recent international policies on peace intervention demonstrate several of the challenges inherent in working to establish a lasting peace after violent conflict.

Traditional state-building, including negotiations, building state institutions, running elections and reconstructing the economy is necessary, but not sufficient for securing peace at the local and community level.

To establish a sustainable peace, it is necessary to combine these "top-down" approaches to peace with local "bottom-up" initiatives. This can often be accomplished through coordination with local civil society organizations that have the benefit of understanding local cultures, social situations, and needs. These organizations are uniquely capable of fostering connections between community members and of opening a dialogue between divided communities.

In societies divided by violent conflict, emotional healing of individuals and of communities proves to be essential for achieving lasting peace, yet international interventions often fail to adequately address this need. This failure allows feelings of anger and hatred to become entrenched.

In the aftermath of violence, interpersonal relationships are severed and anger becomes pervasive as people who had once lived as neighbors often become enemies. The processes of dehumanization and deligitimization make this possible by allowing enemies to see one another as inhuman. Subsequently, the perceived differences between conflicting communities become magnified and people are no longer seen as individuals.

To achieve reconciliation under these circumstances, peace-building programs must address the deeply embedded emotional effects of the conflict on both individuals and communities. This means fostering feelings of forgiveness, understanding and empathy which will help to rebuild interpersonal relationships damaged by the conflict both within and between communities.

In post-conflict societies, it is difficult to achieve true emotional healing because of the long-term commitment these initiatives require. Many societies instead often settle into a fragile state of coexistence which prevents the development of a lasting peace and places the community at risk for future violence. For this reason, peace-building initiatives should strive to incorporate methods that address long-term emotional healing within post-conflict societies.

In order to adequately address the specific needs of post-conflict societies such as Libya, a variety of methodologies must be combined. Initially this would involve participant observation within relevant Libyan communities as a way to become familiar with these communities and their needs. This would be followed by individual interviews with various community members (from both sides of the conflict) to gain further insight into the local concerns, desires and ideas. Additionally, if appropriate, focus groups could also be utilized to gain information and also to foster connections with the community and encourage further community participation. Each of these techniques should be carried out using a combination of collaborative and multidisciplinary methodologies.

By utilizing teams of expert advisors, local professionals and community members, these programs can ensure better access to these communities and the establishment of more relevant and comprehensive programs.

Once background information has been collected, peace-building programs can be developed to address the various needs of post-conflict societies. Throughout analysis of the issues surrounding peace-building in conflict-divided communities, several themes have emerged that should be taken into account.

The first of these is the need for interventions to consider the specific context of the conflict and any social realities that have contributed to it and its aftermath. Although political and physical violence like that seen in Libya proves to be most visible and easily recognizable, less visible forms, such as structural and social violence, prove to be no less important and should also be explored. This involves considering the historical context and underlying social realities, such as post-colonialism and social inequalities, that contribute to violence. Next, these programs should focus upon the needs of local communities in addition to national reconstruction so that local actors, their voices and experiences can help shape the character and focus of these programs. To achieve this, initiatives should collaborate with local professionals and civil society organizations that understand local needs and have access to and credibility within the target communities. Additionally, to ensure that they are relevant to and respectful of their target audiences, these peace-building strategies should incorporate and respect local customs and beliefs. Finally, peace-building must focus upon long-term results in order to achieve a truly sustainable peace. Although short-term programs prove easier to evaluate, they have not been successful in establishing an enduring peace.

Taking each of these four themes into consideration, proposed peace and reconciliation initiatives utilize a multidimensional model for addressing post-conflict communities. Prendergast and Plumb (2002) have identified multiple types of initiatives that can form the basis for these types of programs in Libya. Their first suggestion is that programs address the psychological trauma experienced by individuals and communities through culturally-appropriate mental health initiatives.

Emotional healing through forgiveness and empathy prove to be essential post-conflict because true healing and progression towards peace cannot occur unless resentments and other negative emotions are properly acknowledged and addressed. To achieve emotional healing, programs must address not only the mental health needs of individuals but also the needs of communities as a whole.

Violent conflict often causes deep fractures within society by damaging interpersonal connections not only between conflicting groups but also within these groups. State violence like that seen in Libya causes fear, alienation and distrust to become part of everyday life. Even after the threat of violence ceases to exist, these feelings and experiences persist, affecting all interpersonal interactions within society. This proves to be problematic because interpersonal connections form an essential foundation for a stable society by providing individuals with a sense of belonging and security.

When violence disrupts this support network, feelings of suspicion, mistrust, fear, anger and hatred become widespread. This atmosphere affects all social interactions both within and between conflicting groups, subsequently alienating individuals from one another and increasing feelings of insecurity. For this reason, emotional healing must be achieved not only through mental health initiatives focused upon individuals, but also through initiatives focused upon fostering trust and strengthening social bonds within and between divided communities. Sustained efforts to rebuild communities will help return feelings of stability, serving as a foundation for future peace efforts. As a renewed sense of connection develops and communities begin to overcome the intense negative emotions and experiences of conflicts, true healing and forgiveness can begin.

Due to the longstanding social divisions Gaddafi encouraged throughout his reign, I expect these considerations will prove essential to any future efforts at establishing a lasting peace.

Communities can begin the process of rebuilding trust and connections through several of the other initiatives Prendergast and Plumb have delineated.

Their second recommendation is the implementation of problem-solving workshops that allow communities to resolve specific issues and conflicts that arise during the rebuilding process.

The third potential initiative would be the development of peace commissions and committees which, though similar to problem-solving workshops, differ in that they focus on developing future strategies for promoting peace rather than addressing specific conflicts that arise.

A fourth option for addressing post-conflict situations involves training local community members in conflict resolution methods so that they can learn to listen to and tolerate perspectives different from their own. To achieve empathy, understanding and forgiveness, people must develop a desire and ability to understand another person's point of view even if they do not agree with it. This is an essential component of emotional healing because a person can only experience empathy once he or she is able to view the "enemy" as an individual with similar human emotions and experiences.

A fifth, similar consideration includes supporting indigenous forms of conflict-resolution and healing which have the benefit of being familiar to local communities and therefore more easily accepted than other techniques may be.

Sixth would be the establishment of community organizations and activities which can promote reconciliation through social engagement of "enemies" in a non-confrontational environment.

Finally, various forms of media can be used to allow these peace-building and reconciliation initiatives to reach a wider audience. Radio, television, online and written forms of media allow programs to gain access to much larger communities than can be done in person. This can be beneficial for spreading peaceful messages that counteract widespread hostility, rumors, misconceptions, and misinformation.

This list of initiatives is certainly not exhaustive but it can serve as a useful guide to the types of multidisciplinary and collaborative programs that can be implemented to deal with post-conflict reconciliation. Due to the fact that every community has different needs and desires, some initiatives may work in some areas while they may be inappropriate in others. For this reason, it remains essential that peace-building programs be tailored specifically to their target communities.

In the case of Libya, multiple tracks are needed to address the ongoing reconstruction, healing and reconciliation needs of this divided country. As demonstrated, traditional peace initiatives often fail to create sustainable solutions for community healing which proves to be problematic because of the considerable damage done to communities and interpersonal relationships by violent conflicts. Taking these failures into consideration, Libyan officials, along with local and international experts and aid organizations, should learn from these failures and develop community-based initiatives in order to increase the likelihood of a successful transition to peace in Libya. Although these initiatives should be tailored specifically to the communities being targeted, they should all take the context of the conflict into consideration, address local needs, incorporate cultural elements, and collaborate with existing groups and structures in these communities.

With these principles as a foundation, peace-building initiatives within Libya can be developed to address psychosocial rehabilitation, support conflict-resolution techniques and promote community-based activities.

These programs can begin the process of rebuilding trust and opening dialogues between communities divided by the conflict. This will serve as an important early step in the process of rebuilding that will set the stage for future peace-building efforts in Libya.

Several questions remain about how to achieve a sustainable solution to the trauma and social divisions experienced throughout Libya: how can these recommendations be incorporated into already existing peace-building programs? how can international and state intervention policies be changed to include these types of community-based initiatives? how can we convince funding institutions to support these programs for the amount of time required to achieve any meaningful change? hopefully, these questions will soon be answered as national and international organizations respond to the urgent need that exists for sustainable community-based programs in post-conflict societies such as Libya.

Fourth Trip

I was lucky to have my wife and daughters join me for my fourth trip to Libya in June of 2012. I was able to work with the Libyan Youth Center and the Austrian NGO Hilfswerk on many projects in Tripoli and cities in the west.

The first national conference on mental health, post-revolution, took place on July 4-5, 2012 in Misrata, under the theme "The Future of Mental Health in Libya", I was honored to chair the conference but I give the credit of its success to my colleagues in Misrata and the conference attendees.

We came up with the following recommendations:

1. Large scale psychosocial educational campaign is needed to combat stigma

2. Work with religious and local healers is important to promote and improve the practices of Islamic mental health

3. Interdisciplinary team approach to mental health is needed

4. Raise the ethical standards of practice for mental health professionals

LIBERATED

5. Start high-quality certification and licensure programs

6. Cooperate with world-class universities and treatment centers to improve the standards of mental health care

7. Unite the many mental health teams working independently throughout the country

8. Include psychosocial units in all government sectors

9. Raise awareness of the important role of psychosocial professionals

10. Prepare and start applying realistic programs that deal with immediate crises with focus on long-term improvement of mental health standards of the country

11. National reconciliation is a topic of top importance and priority

12. Psychosocial professionals cannot engage in interrogation or torture procedures

13. Increase the number of inpatient units, and in other cities than Tripoli and Benghazi

14. Focus on issues of PTSD, addiction and violence; and create programs for children

15. Involve children with special needs in public schools and community centers

16. Apply play and art therapy techniques with school children

17. Provide parks, playgrounds and other avenues for relaxation and healing

18. Work with international NGOs but encourage healing Libya through Libyan hands

19. Increase salaries for mental health professionals especially those willing to work in rural and underserved areas

20. Start anonymous hotline for psychosocial support and consultation

21. Exchange ideas and expertise between teams to prevent replicating efforts and reinventing the wheel

22. Revise academic curricula and focus on practical and hands-on aspects

23. Encourage the use of technology, psychological testing and mental health research

24. Provide opportunities for staff improvement through attending courses, CME activities and conferences inside and outside of Libya

LIBERATED

25. Start a national database to track admissions, discharges and medication dispense, also work towards inpatient units in general medical hospitals and open outpatient clinics and day treatment programs to reduce stigma and improve access to services.

To Forgive
Does Not Mean To Forget

I wonder if deep inside each one of us there might be a darker side, an aspect of our personality that we do not feel comfortable confronting or even acknowledging. Not sure where exactly does this discomfort stem from. Some say that it is our insecurity, that we do not think that we are good enough, smart enough or worthy of the blessings that come our way. Others argue that it is our ignorance, that we show a harsher or a hostile side, we shut down, or go to extremes when faced with the unknown, either it be a different color, religion, belief or point of view. Others blame lack of communication, and that all misconceptions and misperceptions will resolve when we open channels with the "other" and start talking with, rather than about, one another. Another group claims that it is our regression when we are lacking a basic need, a child becomes irritable when angry or soiled, a teenager who is bullied might now be seen as defiant or withdrawn because they lack a sense of belonging or self-worth, an adult also regresses when going through caffeine-withdrawal, or a bad night of sleep. So how about lack of security?

LIBERATED

We tend to regress our own styles either internally or externally ranging from bed-wetting, nail-biting, clinginess, all the way to complete shut-down, self-harm or aggression towards others.

I wonder however if it is our pride and arrogance, that when we justify a position we take, or hold to an opinion we adopt, that we dismiss the other or even his existence altogether, because we fear that we might be wrong.

Is it then the fear or the lack of will to communicate with the "other" and listen to a different point of view, or a combination of all of the above?

This is a brainstorming attempt aims to shed some light on the roots of the current chaotic situation in Libya and the struggle of its people.

The dust had settled after very ugly and heavy four decades and an extremely exhausting and bloody war, the wounds left behind are very deep, inflamed, infected and profusely bleeding. It is a sad reality that hundreds of thousands were forced to exile or were imprisoned, executed, raped or tortured, and many ended up killing one another fighting or defending Gaddafi, and many more lost their extremities, homes, schools, jobs, futures and psychosocial support network, all Libyans are in dire need for healing, recovery, rehabilitation and reintegration, a huge task indeed but a very worthy deed.

The chaos and violence that had declared Libya from a role-model to a failing state and turned many fighters to mercenaries and armed militants, is a scenario that could have been prevented or at least reduced if people just listened to pleas and recommendations of Libyan psychosocial experts. Unfortunately, in Libya everybody claims to be an expert and wants to be the boss, the Libyan soup tastes awful because of the too many chefs who have no idea how to taste not alone cook.

Libya will heal only through Libyan hands, her children know the language, religion, culture and customs and they care without having hidden agendas.

Stories of abuse by the abused, and bully by the bullied are heart-breaking. What happens to you can explain your behavior but can never excuse or justify it, wrong is always wrong and right is always right, no matter what the circumstances are. Killing or hurting another is morally and ethically unacceptable. Children should not pay for their parents' crimes and a woman should not be touched just because her husband raped other women.

Many in Libya are suffering in silence, the issue of rape, sexual violence against men and women, or using electric shock on genitals are disgusting practices but are also realities that we need to face not shy away from, we can no longer hide our heads in the sand, stuff our skeletons in the closet or swipe our dirt under the rug, our closets are full they are about to explode, our laundry is dirty but we cannot clean it unless we admit that it is dirty, there is nothing wrong about exposing what happened, the first step towards recovery is to admit that we have a problem. Lack of

LIBERATED

insight is a poor prognostic sign.

I hold the many governments post-Gaddafi responsible before Allah and their people for every child, woman, fighter, amputee, displaced, missing, prisoner, and injured person who continues to suffer. Libya is an extremely rich country and we deserve the best humane treatment and highest clinical standards of care, we just need people who care.

Reconciliation is a word that brings about lots of emotions, controversy and debate in Libya every time it is mentioned, people think it means to forget what happens or simply forgive. Reconciliation is way bigger than just that, it means that the abuser will admit fault, get a fair trial, get an adequate punishment or get forgiven and reintegrated. To forgive has nothing to do with your abuser and everything to do with you, you forgive to let go of the pain and hurt because anger is literally a paralyzing and defeating force and a heavy load to keep carrying around.

Libyans need to be consulted about the best way they see fit to pursue reconciliation, asking someone's opinion and participation empowers them, we want to let Libyans know that they are not broken, we do not "fix" people, no one wants us to fight their fight or walk their walk, they are simply asking for a caring soul, a listening ear and a hand they can hold and shoulder they can lean or cry on along the way.

We know from experience that when someone is threatened they tend to regress, children show that when they wet their beds, cling to others, suck their thumbs, start stuttering or beg to sleep next to their parents, but communities do it through alienating and dehumanizing the other. Many small communities in Libya are glued together in a tribal or political affiliation. When the enemy was one, Libya was a united front, now it seems like we have many Libyas, and that I am afraid can be explained by the small Gaddafi in every one of us, and that Libyans only killed the tree not its roots and got rid of the snake not its venom.

Liberated

A JOURNEY of HOPE & HEALING

Children & War

War and killing are very ugly concepts even when "necessary", their negative impact stays forever in its witness. Children are more vulnerable as they tend to blame themselves for what happens to others, and because in order for a child to develop a healthy personality they need to believe that the world is a safe place and that adults can be trusted.

In Libya, the children's worlds were shattered, they need to be tended to with care and love, they need to know that they are not to be blamed, that what they are experiencing are normal reactions to an abnormal situation, that they are not alone, that they are not crazy, and that adults are around to take care of them and hopefully prevent them for getting hurt again.

Children who witness death, rape, intimidation, abuse and torture can struggle with many negative reactions that can be confusing to them and their caregivers, hence the importance of psycho-education.

Adults need to lead by example so children do not grow up thinking that violence is an acceptable way to resolve conflict. Journaling feelings, writing, acting, drawing, painting and physical activities are very important to release the negative tension and to regain some sense of control, normalcy, routine and structure in their lives.

Adults need to encourage their children to live in "the here and now", that they can learn from their past but focus on improving their current present situation and work towards a brighter future.

For example, we can ask the child to think of a safety plan, family contacts, things to do in case of emergency, think of hobbies or fun activities, non-violent ways to resolve conflict, how to get answers to questions, how to treat others, ways to engage in community service, write letters to those who died or got injured, etc.

Here is some of the advice I gave to caregivers that they found extremely helpful:

1. Attentively listening to children's concerns and trying to alleviate them honestly
2. Having a safety plan in case of emergency
3. Spending extra time with the child, like few extra minutes at bedtime
4. Going back to routine as soon as safely possible
5. Every question and reaction needs to be accommodated

6. Correcting negative behavior through non-violent means
7. Adults should have self-monitoring and discipline, physical punishment of a child is seen as an adult temper tantrum
8. Pointing the child to healthy coping mechanism in them and the environment
9. Spending some time to do bonding family activities.
10. Referring to a specialist when needed, like when the child has prolonged symptoms of anxiety, sorrow, anger, or grief, if their academic and social performance is declining, if they suffer from recurrent nightmares or night-terrors, if they are hallucinating or having paranoid or obsessive thoughts, if they have thoughts to harm themselves or others, if they isolate or self-neglect, if they start to use alcohol or substance, if they have severe psychosomatic symptoms like migraines and startle seizures, if they regress in age like bed-wetting, thumb-sucking, stuttering, or clinging, and if they are suicidal or homicidal, or have access to weapons or lethal means.

LIBERATED

Some of the art/play therapy activities I used successfully with the children in Misrata and other Libyan cities incorporated themes of team-work, self-esteem, respect, brainstorming, anti-bullying, with children hobbies and strengths, with cultural and religious massages like taking care of one's body and cleanliness, respecting elders, tolerating differences, turning to God for strength (some people were very angry at God for allowing things to go sour). Through drawing pictures, coloring, painting, clay and sand, toys and songs, psycho-drama, role-playing, etc, the topic of psychosocial support was introduced in a very benign and non-threatening way.

Challenges

Many questions come to mind when reflecting on the Libyan revolution and war:

1. **A question I get frequently asked is "was it worth it"?**

I know that many people are apprehensive and hesitant to support the Arab revolutions, which I believe is a scandal, we cannot just sit and watch when children and civilians are being killed, injustice anywhere is threat to justice everywhere. Many claim that Libya is a failed state and that it became a safe haven for "terrorists". Libya is experimenting with the meanings of dignity, freedom and democracy, all are brand new values that take time to master.

Given the severe trauma and the combination of weapons and drugs, I think Libya is doing okay and hopefully with the right people in power it will be back on the right track in the near future.

Some still claim that the Gaddafi's era was safer and they dream that his children will resume power, it is true that there was a false sense of safety and security during the previous regimen because people were controlled with fire and iron fist and there was

LIBERATED

an absolute control, new Libya cannot magically get better overnight, it is the responsibility of every one of us.

2. Another question is about who the fighters are and what do they want?

The ones I met in the frontlines are decent civilians who were forced to fight, kill or get hurt, they are asking for basic human rights of freedom and dignity and they are asking for the sacrifices of their colleagues to be honored through achieving the goals of the revolution.

In the midst of the heavy fighting I did not come across any of the new thugs like ISIS.

3. Also what should happen to Gaddafi's supporters?

Libya is a country of six million people and we need everyone to build the country together.

Those who killed or raped need to be brought to justice through the right channels, then we all need to grieve and heal together and move forward. If we continue to force those who supported Gaddafi to live in isolation and exile and continue to treat them with hatred and revenge, then they will in few years or decades decide to start another "revolution" and cause lots of bloodshed, a heavy price that Libya cannot afford.

4. The role and rights of countries that helped Libya is another issue.

Those who believed in doing right and helped Libya without an agenda need to be thanked and appreciated, but those who look at Libya as a piece of cake do not deserve any of my respect and have not learned the lesson that Libyans know how to fight.

Liberated
A JOURNEY of HOPE & HEALING

Now What?

Gaddafi promised a very long and exhausting war even after his death. He meant a psychosocial war that breeds hate and anger between neighboring tribes, cities and across generations.

The need to understand Post-Traumatic Stress Disorder (PTSD) and mental health comorbidities has never been greater in the Middle East than now. The spread of the "Arab Spring" revolutions throughout the region has resulted in atrocities and the rise of psychiatric problems. Libya is no exception. This country was under siege by a unitarian regime for over forty years with one of the worst healthcare systems in the region. There is no clear infrastructure for medical or mental health care. Another peculiar circumstance for Libya is the need for a full fledge war to achieve the liberation of the country. The above makes Libya a country that presents a wonderful opportunity for improving the delivery and provision of medical and mental healthcare services.

For the past forty-two years the country has been ruled by a totalitarian regime, an era referred to by many as the darkest years of Libya's tumultuous history. Under the rule of dictatorship, Libyans suffered with no adequate education, social services, or healthcare leading the Libyan people into despair.

As for mental health pre-revolution, Libya had only two hospitals (asylums), one in Tripoli and another in Benghazi. The standards of care in the hospitals were extremely poor; the use of old medications, treatment modalities and at times unethical practices was common. The role of mental health professionals was misunderstood and made fun of, and psychiatric symptoms were attributed to the act of magic or evil eye and treated through "traditional local healers".

Already in a precarious position, the 2011 Libyan revolution gave Libyans hope for a change, but came at a very heavy price. The war lasted for many years with tens of thousands of people dead and hundreds of thousands injured and displaced. Fighting is still an ongoing daily occurrence in cities like Benghazi. The medical and mental toll on the Libyan people became overwhelming, complicated by the lack of standard medical and mental healthcare in the country as well as the cultural stigma to accessing the sparse mental health services.

According to the Libyan Ministry of Health there is only one psychiatrist per every 200,000 Libyans making the mental health situation even more difficult to assess and treat. Add this to the already desperate and growing issue of medical health care, the comorbid states of PTSD and other medical ailments will significantly increase throughout the country.

Currently in Libya, it is estimated that there are tens

of thousands of cases of PTSD ranging from children and adults to military personnel, physicians, first responders and so forth. From my previous multiple visits to Libya since the start of the revolution in February of 2011, it is clear that there is not a single corner of the country that has not been negatively affected by the war. Unfortunately, due to the lack of mental health care in the country and the lack of professionally-trained trauma mental health workers, the cases of PTSD will continue to linger and perhaps grow adding to the already bleak situation.

The only "advantage" of the war is that Libyans are grieving together and leaning on one another for support, they are more willing to discuss the mental health impact of the war and accept psychosocial support.

In my professional opinion, Libya needs many decades for its psychological wounds to completely heal.

Some of the most important elements of psychosocial recovery in Libya are included in my project Libya Al-Shefa:

1. Psycho-social education: through conducting TV, radio and online programs, distributing leaflets and running lectures, seminars and workshops

LIBERATED

2. Capacity-building of Libyan mental health professionals through training-of-trainers courses on trauma-focused interventions and therapies

3. Establishing trauma assistance hotline

4. Opening day treatment programs and psycho-social educational and resources centers

5. Conducting peer support groups for women, fighters and families of the deceased on both sides of the conflict

6. Conducting training and hands-on activities on play and art therapy techniques for children, with teachers, social workers and volunteers from Libyan non-governmental organizations

7. Conducting community brainstorming workshops and activities on peace and reconciliation

The Wounded Healer

The 2011 war in Libya resulted in the country's liberation but that came at a very heavy psychosocial price. The numbers of those impacted by the mental health consequences of the war (ranging from depression and grief to addiction and post-traumatic stress disorder) are estimated to be in the tens of thousands.

One sector of society that is usually resistant to admit to the impact of witnessing or hearing the trauma story is the healers' group.

War is ugly and it leaves heavy and long lasting imprints on the psyche of all involved. Many Libyans did not enjoy their victory due to their daily struggle with memories of their dead loved ones. Healers are no exception.

Self-care is vital to prevent provider burnout (compassion fatigue/vicarious trauma). You cannot care for others unless you take care of yourself first. Healers need to know their limits and be assertive and mindful not to carry a load heavier than what they can realistically handle.

Liberated

A JOURNEY of HOPE & HEALING

Academic Detachment

One of the most fascinating defense mechanisms that professionals use in order to cope with or shield self from traumatic stories shared by clients is referred to as academic distancing or detachment.

The therapist should empathically share aspects of the trauma with the storyteller but without losing the therapeutic distance. Therapists can achieve such self-protective skill through training and experience.

Trauma survivors can trigger strong feelings in gentle therapists that could render them vulnerable to compassion fatigue.

Some therapists do journal, not only their feelings but also thoughts, behaviors and every day's events in order to process confusing aspects of the trauma.

I found academic writing (reports, articles, blogs, and children story series) about the Libyan revolution to be not only protective or useful but also a rewarding endeavor that helped me a great deal come into terms with painful firsthand events and vicarious traumatic aspects of the war and its aftermath.

Academic detachment especially through writing and artistic expressions is a skill that I do highly rec-

LIBERATED

ommend every trauma expert should try to master, as it could serve as a very useful tool in preventing or reducing burnout and in maximizing the trauma responder's benefit potential.

Conclusion

The good news is that humans are resilient even in the face of terror, and Libyans have what it takes to recover from their painful recent past, heal the invisible wounds of trauma and rebuild their country. If things continue going in the right direction, Libya might indeed become a role model in every standard including mental health care. That however requires the perseverance and hard work of many good people who care deeply about their country.

It is my hope and dream to continue to help my people in their long struggle for freedom and democracy, to try to ease their pain and suffering, to be a frontline soldier in their psychological war and be an instrumental player in their journey of healing, recovery, peace and hope.

May Libya continue to inspire the world, and may Allah the almighty God bless the beautiful country of Libya.

Liberated
A JOURNEY *of* HOPE & HEALING

References

Restorative Justice

Anderson, Lisa. (2011). *Demystifying the Arab Spring: Parsing the Differences between Tunisia, Egypt, and Libya*. Foreign Affairs, 90(3),2-7.

Baba, Marietta L. (2000). *Theories of Practice in Anthropology: A Critical Appraisal.* NAPA Bulletin, 18,17-45.

Dunne, Michele. (2011). *Libya's Revolution: Do Institutions Matter?* Current History, 110 (740), 370-371.

Gilsenan, Michael. (2002). *On Conflict and Violence.* Jeremy MacClancy (Ed.), *Exotic No More: Anthropology on the Front Lines* (Pp. 99-113). Chicago: University of Chicago Press.

Halpern, Jodi and Harvey M. Weinstein. (2004). *Rehumanizing the Other: Empathy and Reconciliation.* Human Rights Quarterly, 26, 561-583.

Hoogenboom, David A. and Stephanie Vieille. (2009). *Rebuilding Social Fabric in Failed States: Examining Transitional Justice in Bosnia*. Human Rights Review, 11, 183-198.

Hutchison, Emma and Roland Bleiker. (2008). *Emotional Reconciliation: Reconstituting Identity and Community after Trauma.* European Journal of Social Theory, 11(3), 385-403.

Kirmayer, Laurence J. (2010). *Peace, Conflict, and Reconciliation: Contributions of Cultural Psychology.* Transcultural Psychiatry, 47(1), 5-19.

Kleinman, Arthur. (2000). *The Violences of Everyday Life: The Multiple Forms and Dynamics of Social Violence.* Veena Das, Arther Kleinman, Mamphele Ramphele and Pamela Reynolds (Eds.), *Violence and Subjectivity* (Pp. 226-241). Berkeley: University of California Press.

Lassiter, Luke E. (2005). *The Chicago Guide to Collaborative Ethnography.* London, UK: The University of Chicago Press.

Lederach, John P. (1997). *Building Peace: Sustainable Reconciliation in Divided Societies.* Washington, D.C.: United States Institute of Peace Press.

Mertus, Julie. (2004). *Improving International Peacebuilding Efforts: The Example of Human Rights Culture in Kosovo*. Global Governance, 10(3), 333-351.

Pouligny, Beatrice, Bernard Doray and Jean-Clement Martin. (2007). *Methodological and Ethical Problems: A Trans-Disciplinary Approach.* Pouligny, Beatrice, Simon Chesterman and Albrecht Schnabel (Eds.), *After Mass Crime: Rebuilding States and Communities* (Pp. 19-40). New York: United Nations University Press.

Prendergast, John and Emily Plumb. (2002). *Building Local Capacity: From Implementation to Peacebuilding*. S.J. Stedman, D. Rothchild and R.M. Cousens (Eds.), *Ending Civil Wars: The Implementation of Peace Agreements* (Pp. 327-349). Boulder, CO: Lynne Rienner Publishers.

Margo G, Bonning B, Neighbor TW. *Focus on Libya: Understanding the Arab Spring from the Inside.* [Internet document available from http://www.world-affairs.org; published Feb 2012].

Topol SA. *The Mad Dog's Madhouse.* Foreign Policy. [Internet document available from: http://www.foreignpolicy.com; Published September 11, 2011]

Hall M. *The trauma of revolution.* [Interbnet document: available from http://psuvanguard.com; published on November 17, 2011].

Elwafi H. Child *Psychiatry in Libya: Helping Children in the Midst of Revolution. Child.* [Internet document: available from http://www.aacp.org]

Zeiton M. *Time to rebuild a "shattered" healthcare system.* [Internet Document: available from http://www.libyaherald.com; Tripoli, 26 June 2012].

Devi S. *Mending mental health in Misrata.* The Lancet 2011; 378 (9803):1618.

Zeiton M. *Extinction by instinct.* [An internet document available from http://www.sadeqinstitute.org; Published May 2012] http://www.plosone.org/article/info%3Adoi%2F10.1371%2Fjournal.pone.0040593http://www.mercycorps.org/countries/libya/25804http://psychnews.psychiatryonline.org/newsarticle.

Liberated
A JOURNEY of HOPE & HEALING

LIBERATED

Notes

A JOURNEY of **HOPE & HEALING**

NOTES

LIBERATED

Notes

A JOURNEY *of* **HOPE & HEALING**

NOTES

LIBERATED

NOTES

A JOURNEY *of* **HOPE & HEALING**

NOTES

رحلة الأمل والشفاء

الملاحظات

رحلة الأمل والشفاء

الملاحظات

رحلة الأمل والشفاء

الملاحظات

رحلة الأمل والشفاء

الملاحظات

رحلة الأمل والشفاء

الملاحظات

رحلة الأمل والشفاء

الملاحظات

رحلة الأمل والشفاء

فى الختام

الشعب الليبى أثبت أنه - رجالًا ونساءًا - كانوا رجالًا فى الحرب، فالمطلوب منهم الآن أن يكونوا رجالًا فى السلم، فالحرب المادية قد انتهت لكن المعركة المعنوية مستمرة وتحتاج إلى نفس طويل وصبر ومثابرة. عزاؤنا أن الله مع الصابرين، شعبنا طيب وعددنا قليل والخير فينا كثير فيجب أن لا نفقد المزيد من شبابنا للإحباط والاكتئاب والإدمان والانتحار، وأملى كبير فى الله أن أرى بلدى الحبيب مشعل هداية وفى مصاف الدول المتقدّمة من جميع النواحى وليس ذلك على الله بعزيز ولا عسير المنال لكن يحتاج أناسًا قلوبهم على ليبيا ينظرون إليها كأم رؤوم لاكبقره حلوب، أملى وحلمى أن أبذل كل جهدى لمساعدة أهلى ورفعة بلدى فى كفاح طويل من أجل العزة والكرامة والبناء والشفاء. أسأله سبحانه أن يجعلنى من جنوده ويستعملنى فى خدمة دينه وحوائج عباده

عاشت ليبيا حرَّةً أبيَّةً جميلةً وباركها اللهُ

ماذا الآن

أهمية فهم اضطراب كرب ما بعد الصدمة وغيره من الآثار النفسية للحرب هى من الضرورات القصوى فى هذه المرحلة من تاريخ ليبيا. وفى الحالة الليبية فإن نظام حكم الفرد الذى استمر أكثر من أربعة عقود وسبّب إهمالًا جسيمًا فى الجوانب النفسية والاجتماعية حيث لا توجد بُنية تحتية وظروف المستشفيات النفسية يندى لها الجبين ولا تنطبق عليها معايير الإنسانية وهذا كما أسلفت قد يهيئ فرص ذهبية لبناء نظام صحى رائع فى ليبيا الجديدة يتعاون فيها الكل فى عملية الشفاء والتعافى و إعادة التأهيل

وصمة العار المرتبطة بطب النفس ومحاولة شرح الأعراض النفسية بتأثير الجن والسحر والعين هى أمور لا زالت شائعه فى مجتمعنا الليبى ، كذلك فإن أساليب العقاب البدنى والعنف الأسرى والتمييز العرقى موجوده عندنا سواءً اعترفنا بذلك أم لا ، والفرصه الآن مواتيه لأن يتغير ذلك كله إلى الأفضل ولأن نرتقى بالانسان الليبى الذىٍ هو من خير أمَّةٍ أخرجت للناس حتى يتحمّل مسئوليته ويكن بحق وجداره خليفة الله فى أرضه

رحلة الأمل والشفاء

سلسلة طفل الثورة الليبية هى محاولة للتعريف بالآثار النفسية والاجتماعية للحرب على ليبيا بطريقة مبسَّطه تستخدم أساليب العلاج باللعب والفن والرواية ، فكما تعلم فبعض الأطفال قد لا يستطيع إما لصغر سنّه او عدم نموّه العمرى أو الذهنى أن يعبّر عن أحاسيسه ومشاعره وأفكاره وربما أعراضه عن طريق الكلام بينما يستطيع ذلك عن طريق التصرفات ، فنوجّه هذا المخزون العاطفى عند الطفل لجوانب ايجابيه تساعده والبالغين القائمين على رعايته على تجاوز مشاعر الخوف والقلق من الأزمة والمجهول ، وهذا أمر بالغ الخطورة والأهمية حيث نتعلم من أحداث ماضينا التعايش مع وقائع حاضرنا والاستعداد لما يحمله مستقبلنا فلا نبقى سجناء الصدمات العنيفة التى مرّت ببلادنا بل نحاول تعلّم دروسها من أجل واقع أفضل ومستقبل أجمل لنا وللأجيال المقبلة

الأطفال والمراهقون بعد الحرب ، وحتى البالغون ، يحتاجون إلى زيادة جسور التواصل والتعبير عن الذات. ثم زيادة وسائل التكيّف مع الأحوال الصادمة وكذلك زيادة شبكتى الدعم النفسى والاجتماعى المحيطة بهم . وعن طريق أنشطه بسيطه كما فى سلسلة طفل الثورة يمكن لأفراد الأسرة الحديث بصراحة مما يعزّز الثقة وينمى شبكة الدعم وهذه الجلسات تعلّم أفراد الأسرة ما يحتاجه كل واحد فيها وكيفية تأقلمه وتكيّفه مما يساعد فى توجيهه لزيادة الإيجابيات ودرء السلبيات أو التقليل منها . هذه الأنشطة كذلك من السهل تعلّمها والتحكم فى مدى تطبيقها وهى أمور مهمه للناجين من الصدمات حيث قد تنشأ عندهم اعتقادات خاطئه بفقدان التحكم وعدم القدرة على التركيز والتعلّم أو أن الحياة يجب أن لا يكون لها طعم بعد فقد الحبيب أو القريب ، فمجرد إجراء انشطه خفيفه قد نستطيع درء حالات الكآبه والإحباط وفقدان الرغبة فى الهوايات وفقد المستقبل وقد نستطيع مساعدة شفاء المجتمع عن طريق التقليل من أعراض الحِداد والحزن واضطراب كرب ما بعد الصدمة وغيرها

رحلة الأمل والشفاء

الشعور بالنبذ الاجتماعي
تشجيع السلوك العدواني من الآخرين باعتباره وسيلة دفاع عن النفس
الشعور بالنقص خصوصًا في الطفل الذي يوصف بصفات السلبية الجسدية أو العقلية

عدم مقدرة الطفل على التعبير بالكلام بسبب تأخّر ذهني أو توحّد وغيرها
الشعور بالإحباط والفشل عند عدم إنجاز ما يريده له البالغون
منع الطفل من تفريغ طاقته كمنعه من الحركة والكلام
تعرّض الطفل للإيذاء والتعذيب والعدوانية من غيره

ومن النصائح الموصّى بها والتي طبّقناها بنجاح في ليبيا

التوقف عن التعامل القاسي، أي عدم الضرب والإهانة
ابعاد الطفل عن مشاهدة النزاعات

ابعاد الطفل عن القدوة السيئة من أصحاب وتلفاز وغيرها ومراقبة أنشطته على الهاتف والإنترنت

زيادة ثقة الطفل بنفسه

تفريغ طاقة الطفل البدنية عن طريق الأنشطة

تشجيع الطفل على التعبير عن نفسه بوسائل مختلفه تناسبه
إشعار الطفل بأهمية ما يفكر به ويفعله

عدم تكليف الطفل أكثر من طاقته
إعطاء رسائل إيجابية للطفل عند كل فرصة سانحه واستخدام جداول تعديل السلوك

عدم توبيخ الطفل أو نقده في الملأ

رحلة الأمل والشفاء

اللجوء إلى المساعدة المهنيّة من المختصين فى الحالات التى تحتاج إلى تحويل وهى الأطفال الذين تستمر عندهم الأعراض الطبيعية للحزن والقلق مدّة ، فبينما أن أغلب الأطفال والمراهقين يتعافون تمامًا من آثار الحرب بمجرد حصولهم على الرعاية والحنان والاهتمام والدعم النفسى ، فإن البعض يحتاج إلى خدمات أكثر تخصّصاً

الأطفال الذين يتأثر مستواهم الدراسى أو علاقاتهم الأسرية والاجتماعية
الخوف الشديد كنوبات الهلع والكوابيس المتكرّرة أو المستمرة

العزلة والانطواء الشديدين كإهمال النظافة الشخصية وفقدان الرغبة فى الأنشطة المحبوبة سابقًا

كثرة الوساوس والأفكار التشاؤمية كقصر المستقبل وسواده ولوم النفس والشعور بالذنب

التفكير فى الانتحار أو إيذاء النفس أو الغير
التوقف عن الأكل

الأعراض الجسمانية القوية كالتشنّج والصداع الشديد
الأعراض العقلية كالهلوسة وشدّة الشك

النكوص العمرى كالتبوّل والتبرّز اللاإرادى والتأتأه ومص الأصابع وقضم الأظافر
العصبيه الزائدة - مايسمّى بالسلوك العدوانى

اقتناء السلاح أو اللجوء إلى الخمرا والمخدّرات
السلوك العدوانى هو من أكثر الشكاوى التى جاءتنى من أولياء الأمور والمدرّسين وما يسمّى السلوك العدوانى هو أى تصرّف سلبى يصدر من الطفل تجاه الآخرين على صورة عنف جسدى أو لفظى ، ومن أسبابه

تقليد الطفل للبالغين أو لأصدقاء أو شخصيات كرتونيه

رحلة الأمل والشفاء

كتابة الأفكار فى مذكّره يوميه هى أيضًا وسيله ناجحه للتنفيس عن المشاعر عدم نشر الإشاعات أو تصديق كل ما يقال ويعرَض فى وسائل الإعلام. البعض يستخدم طريق الجدول الآتى فى نقل الأخبار

هل الخبر صادق	نعم	نعم	لا	لا
هل من المفيد إعادة نشره	نعم	لا	نعم	لا

من النصائح التى حاولت تقديمها طرق حماية الأطفال أثناء الحروب والأزمات عن طريق

تقليل تعريضهم للتلفاز ومناظر القتل والدماء والدمار
الاستماع إلى الطفل باهتمام فكل سؤال فى فترة الحرب وحتى فى غيرها سؤال عادل ويحتاج جوابًا عادلاً ، ومن المهم لزرع ثقة الطفل بنفسه وتقوية شخصيته اشعاره بأهمية رأيه واحترام تفكيره

منح الأطفال الشعور بالاطمئنان كالاسعافات النفسية الأولية ووضع خطط طوارئ منح الأطفال وقتًا واهتمامًا إضافيًا عن طريق المشاركة والاستماع خاصةً ما قبل النوم

العودة إلى ممارسة الأنشطة السابقة وروتين ما قبل الحرب بأسرع ما يمكن إذا توافرت السلامة

توقّع واحترام تصرف الطفل وردَّة فعله وتقويم السلبى منها
مراقبة السلوك الشخصى للبالغين فهم القدوة التى يراها الطفل فيتعلم منها
توجيه الطفل إلى موارد التأقلم الذاتية عنده وأسرته ومحيطه كهواياته المحبّبة
تشجيع النشاط الجماعى فى البيت لتقوية الروابط الأسريه وفتح جسور الحوار والتواصل

رحلة الأمل والشفاء

كذلك من المهم أن نعيش فى ال (هنا) و (الآن) أى فى الحاضر فنسأل الأطفال عن واقعهم اليومى وشعورهم بالأمان ومشاكلهم الحالية ، نعرّج قليلًا على الماضى فنصحّح المفاهيم الخاطئة عنه ثم نركّز على كيفية الاستعداد للمستقبل فى حال التعرّض - لا سمح الله لمثل الأحداث التى مرّت على البلاد من جديد
أمثلة على التركيز الواقعى والتفكير المستقبلى

ماهى الثلاثة أشياء التى يمكن أن تفعلها لوحدك أو مع أفراد عائلتك للحفاظ على سلامتكم فى حال حدوث خطر جديد

ماهى الأشياء التى سأعملها اليوم لأحافظ على روتينى المعتاد
ماهى خطّة الأمان -المكان والمعدّات- التى اتفّق عليها أفراد الأسرة
ماهى بعض الطرق لفض النزاعات بأسلوب غير عنيف
ماهى الأسئلة التى لا أعرف لها إجابة ويمكن أن أسأل عنها أحد البالغين الذين أثق بهم

هذه بعض النصائح التى استطيع تطبيقها عندما أكون غاضبًا أو خائفًا
بعض الناجين من الصدمات وجدوا راحة بال ومساعده ذاتيه فى النصائح الآتية
كتابة رسائل لأسر الشهداء أو أطقم الإسعاف
المشاركة فى مشاريع مجتمعيه مفيده كالتطوع مع الهلال الأحمر أو حملات النظافة

تلوين حائط احتفالى لتخليد ذكرى المتوفّين
جمع تبرعات لمساعدة المحتاجين

كتابة تقارير أو مقالات عن الحرب وكيفية تطبيق وسائل المساعدة الذاتية فيها كالأكل الصحى والنوم الصحى والابتعاد عن التدخين والمخدّرات
الاتجاه لوسائل صحيه للتكيّف كما فى الصلاة والرياضه وزيادة الشبكات الاجتماعية

معنى الحرب عند الأطفال

الحرب والقتل شيئ بغيض -كُتب عليكم القتال وهو كُره لكم-حتى في حالة الضرورة حيث إن أعراضها السلبية كثيرة من موت وتدمير وفساد. يجب أن يعلم الأطفال أن ما حصل ليس لهم ذنب فيه وأن من مات ليسوا هم سبب ذلك، منهم بحكم عدم نضج عقلياتهم قد يلومون النفس في حالة الحداد مما يترتب عليه اكتئاب وانطواء وأحيانًا تفكير بالانتحار، وكذلك يجب أن يعلموا الأعراض الطبيعية للحوادث الغير طبيعية التي مرّوا بها كالخوف والقلق والتوتّر كما في حالة سماع الأصوات العالية أو مشاهدة مناظر دماء وإيذاء قد تتكرر عندهم في صور كوابيس وهلع ورعب ليلي أو تبوّل لا إرادي. فبمجرد أن نشرح طبيعة هذه الأعراض والطرق الصحيّة للتكيف معها لولي الأمر والمسئول عن الطفل فأننا نسدي خدمة كبرى للطفل حيث يتفهمه البالغون ويحاولون دعمه مما يقلّل هذه الأعراض ويمنع مشاكل أسريه قد تؤثر في شخصية الطفل وتهزها أو تصبغها بطابع العدوانية، وكذلك من المهم منع الرصاص العشوائي والإحتفالي، وإعطاء القدوة الصالحة للطفل حتى لا يعتقد أن العنف ضروري لفض النزاعات مما قد يولد عنده نزعه أو نزوة إجراميّة، من المهم للطفل أيضًا معرفة أنه ليس وحيدًا في معاناته بل هناك آلاف في مثل موقفه، فالشعور بالوحدة والعزله قاتل
بعض الأطفال كذلك قد يضطر للنزوح أو التهجير أو ينتقل إلى مدرسة أخرى أو يكون قد فقد أصدقاء أو أقارب فمن المهم إعطائهم مساحة للتعبير عن مشاعر الفقد والحداد والإحتفاء بالميت عن طريق تخليد ذكرياته الحلوة والحكي عن مشاعر الغضب تجاه الفقيد وتجاوزها إن وُجِدت، ويمكنهم كتابة رسائل إلى الشهداء مثلا

الانسلاخ الأكاديمي

إحدى وسائل الدفاع السيكولوجي الشيّقة لحماية النفس من آثار الصدمة سواءً المشاهدة أو المسموعة هي كتابة المشاعر والتجارب كمحاولتي في هذا الكتاب. المعالج قد يتأثر بالنواحي المؤلمه من القصص التي يسمعها، لكن عليه لحماية نفسه من الاحتراق الذاتي أن لا يفقد حدوده المهنيّة وهذا فن يحتاج وقتًا لإتقانه

وكلما كان المعالج حنونًا أو مشاركًا في بعض الجوانب للناجي من الصدمة كلّما كان تأثره أكبر. ورأينا مفعول ذلك علينا معاشر المعالجين الليبييّن فإن فرحتنا بليبيا لم تطُل حيث رأينا الدمار النفسي والاجتماعي. نراه في دموع الأمهات الثكالى وآهات الأرامل واليتامى وفي مقعد الأحبّة الخالي في رمضان والمواسم والأعياد

بالنسبه لي فإن كتابة يومياتي في ليبيا ثم اختزال الأحداث التي عاصرتها في هذا الكتاب ومجموعة قصص للأطفال، وكذلك إعطائي للمحاضرات والمداخلات عن ليبيا وثورتها كلها وسائل تنفيس وشفاء ذاتي لجراحي واضطراب كرب ما بعد الصدمة الذي أعانيه والذي لا أبيعه بمال الدنيا فهو بالنسبه لي بلدي الحبيب وشهداؤها وصوت أمي

رحلة الأمل والشفاء

احد متطوعى الهلال الأحمر المصراتى حضر لتمثيل دور الثائر فى إحدى الدورات التدريبية للأخصائيين النفسيّين إلا أنه لم يستطع مواصلة وإكمال الجلسة حيث أغرقته دموعه وذكريات ومشاهد الدماء والأجسام المحترقة والأشلاء المقطّعة التى اضطر لحملها ودفنها

مما سبق نعلم أن الحرب قبيحه ولها تأثير ثقيل وطويل الأمد على النفسية لكل من رآها أو شارك فيها فليس سهلًا أن تقتل إنسانًا أو تراه أمامك مقتولًا. فلابد للمعالج الجريح من الاهتمام بنفسه ومعرفة حدوده حتى لا يحمل ما هو فوق طاقته مما قد يؤدى للاحتراق الذاتى

المعالج الجريح

الحرب فى ليبيا كانت نتيجتها طيّبة لكن ضريبتها باهظه من الناحية النفسية والاجتماعيه فالحرب لم تدع بيتًا إلا دخلته

من الشرائح التى عادةً إمّا تُخفى أو تنفى أو تتجاهل الآثار النفسية شريحة المعالجين وسأعطى بعض الأمثلة لتوضيح هذه النقطة

فى حالتى أنا فإنّ مكالمتى مع الوالدة وكذلك مقتل محمّد نبّوس وابنى خالتى أثّر فيّ كثيرًا ولازال

أحد الأخصائيين النفسيّين فى مصراته يحمل غضبًا شديدًا على أهل تاورغاء وقال أنه لايرغب فى علاج ولا الحديث مع ولاحتى رؤية أحد من تاورغاء

أحد أطباء العظام من مصراته فقد أخويه فى معركة تاورغاء، كان هذا الطبيب يعمل فى أحد مستشفيات بنغازى وقد اهتمّ بمريضة تاورغيه وأكرمها، فتعجّبت من حسن أخلاقه ورفعة معاملته واندهشت أكثر عند سماع قصّته

أحد الأخصائيين النفسيّين من بنغازى ذهب مع الثوار حتى معركة سرت التى قُتل فيها القذافى ورأى الكثير من زملائه يموت أمامه. ظن أن ذلك لم يؤثّر فيه حتى اشترك فى دورة تدريب وكان يمثّل دور الثائر، فعلم حينها عن طريق دموعه أنه لازال يحمل آلامه وذكرياته فى قلبه

رحلة الأمل والشفاء

تساؤل آخر عن دور الأجانب وحقوقهم الآن علينا، ولا ينكر الفضل إلا قليل الأصل فقد ساعدتنا دول شقيقه وصديقه وكثير منهم فعلوا ما أملاه عليهم الضمير العالمي من إيقاف مجازر ونصرة مستضعفين، ولكن بعضهم فعل ذلك ليس لسواد عيون ليبيا وإنما من أجل مصالح شخصية ومآرب وأطماع، فالبعض رأى ليبيا كبقره حلوب وككعكه حلوه تستحق التقسيم وهؤلاء يقال لهم موتوا بغيظكم واخسئوا فالشعب الليبي لايتوسل ولايتسوّل وليبيا ليست للبيع ولا للتقسيم. من ساعدنا يُذكر ويُشكر ومن أراد لنا أن نرجع إلى ذُل واستعمار فهو لم يتعلم الدرس فنحن شعب لغير الله لانركع

أخيرًا يتساءل الكثير في قلق وترقّب عن طول المدّة التي تحتاجها البلاد للاستقرار وهذا سؤال عادل يحتج إلى إجابة عادلة. هذه الإجابة موجود جزء منها عند كل واحد منّا فعلينا كلنا أن تتوقف إجابته، فإذا رأينا أن كل منا راع ومسئول عن رعيته وجندي من جنود هذا الدين يخدم ليبيا بكل صدق وإخلاص عَندها يلتئم الشمل وتشفى الجراح ويعود منظر البيت أجمل مما كان

خلاصة كلامي أنني متفائل بشدّه وسأظل حتى آخر يوم في عمري، وإن لم نستطع تحقيق كل أحلامنا فلا مانع أن نحاول تحقيق بعضها ولن يحول بيننا وبين محاولة مساعدة ليبيا على الشفاء إلا الموت وما أحلاها شهادة في سبيل الله والوطن. أحاول الآن بشتى الطرق العودة النهائية إلى بلدي الحبيب للقيام بمشاريع كثيرة نفسية واجتماعية من أجل الشفاء وإعادة التأهيل وإصلاح ذات البين، والله أسأل أن يوفّقني لهذا في أسرع وقت ممكن وأن يجعلني مفتاحًا للخير مغلاقا للشر كفيلًا لليتامي والأرامل وأن يستعملني في خدمة العباد وعمارة البلاد وأسأله سبحانه صدقا في القول وإخلاصًا في العمل وقبولًا منه ابتغاء وجهه الكريم وما توفيقي إلا بالله عليه توكّلت وإليه أنيب

رحلة الأمل والشفاء

السؤال الأخر عن ماهية الثّوار ومطالبهم، والثائر فى نظرى هو من ثار فى وجه الظلم وثار فى وجه بقايا آثاره فساهم فى تنظيم البلاد ونظافتها وأمنها فالدور لم يتم بل هو مستمر إنما تمّ توجيهه من الثورة إلى الدولة. ومطالب الثوار الحقيقيين الذى رأيتهم فى الجبهات وجلست معهم فى اللقاءات وقضيت معهم أجمل الأوقات هم إخوة رائعون وأخوات مطالبهم عادله مشروعه وبسيطة يريدون احترام دماء الشهداء بتحقيق الأمن ثم العدل ثم الاستقرار فالبناء فالرفاهية

تساؤل آخر هو عن كيفية التعامل مع مؤيدى النظام السابق. وهنا رأيى المتواضع أنه من زياراتى لمستشفيات وسجون ليبيا خلال الحرب وبعدها رأيت فرقا بين معاملة الجريح الثائر وجريح الكتائب ورأيت أسرى لمدة طويلة دون محاكمة. أخلاق هذه الثورة هى معاملة الجريح بالحسنى والأسير بالرفق والعدل حتى وقت محاكمته، فما لا نريده هو أن من حُبس أو عُذب أو هُجِّر سيكره هذه الثوره وسيقوم بثورةٍ مضاده إما الآن أو بعد سنين أو عقود وهذا ما لانريده لليبيانا الحبيبه فجراحها تكفيها، نريد احتواء من تاب منهم توبة نصوحا ومناصحة من لازال يتمنى عودة النظام السابق، نريد كلمة سواء وأن نسمع من الطرفين عسى أن يأتى الله بالصلح والصلح خير

تساؤل آخر عن المقيمين فى الخارج وهنا يحضرنى أمران، أحدهما أن مئات الآلاف من الليبيين موجودون الآن خارجها إما لأنهم كانوا مع النظام السابق أو لأسباب أخرى، وهذا أمر محزن فليبيا عدد سكانها قليل وتحتاج كل ابنائها، وأتمنى أنه مستقبلاً يكون خروج الليبيين إلى بلدان أخرى هو فقط لغرض السياحة فالبنيه التحتية والدراسية والعمّالية يجب أن تتحسن فى ليبيا لمصاف الدول المتقدمة فلا يكون هناك داع عند أبنائها لهجرها فالغربة مُرّة ولاينبئّك مثل خبير. والأمر الثانى أنه لا فضل لليبيّ الخارج عن ليبيّ الداخل ولا العكس فالكل إخوة ؛ ورغم احترامي وتقديري لكل من رجع إلى ليبيا خلال الحرب وبعدها من أجل المساهمة فى تحريرها وبنائها إلا أن هذا واجب علينا وحقّ مشروع لأمّنا الحبيبة لانتجمّل به ولايزايد أحدنا على الآخر، ولا أرى أنه من الإنصاف أن تدّعى البطولة برجوعك إلى بلدك فى وقت احتياجتك فيه أو ذهابك لرؤية أهلك عندما كان خطر الموت يحدق بهم

32

تساؤلات

تجربتى فى ليبيا قبل الحرب وخلالها وبعدها تثير فىّ عدة تساؤلات أطرحها على قرائى الأحبّة عسى أجد شفاءًا من بعض جراحاتى فى أذان مصغيه أو قلوبٍ مهتمّه سؤالى الأول طُرح علىّ فى إحدى اللقاءات الإذاعية فى الولايات المتّحدة يوم مقتل السفير الأمريكى فى بنغازى ، وهو الثمن الباهظ للثورة وهل كانت تستحق كل هذه التضحيات ،بالطبع هم متخوفون مما يسمونه بالمد الإسلامى والتيار الدينى ويحاولون عدم التدخّل فى الأزمة برغم رؤية مناظر تدمى القلب وتدمع العين. جوابى أن الثورة تستحق الموت من أجلها ولكن ليبيا أيضًا تستحق أن تعيش وتزدهر ، نحن لم نختر طريق الموت ، بدأناها سلميه وتم فرض تسليحها علينا، البعض يقول أن ما تغير هو فقط العَلم والنشيد وأن فترة القذّافى كانت أفضل من ناحية الأمان والتنظيم وهذا كلام به قليل حق يراد به كثير باطل فالقبضه الحديدية للنظام السابق كانت تعطى انطباعًا كاذبًا بالأمن والنظام فلما زال رأينا كيف أن البلاد تفتقر إلى أدنى مقوّمات العيش الكريم ، وليس من العدل أن نعتقد أن ليبيا ستتغير بين ليلة وضحاها إلى جنّة الله فى أرضه ولكن ليس من العدل أيضًا أن نرى حكومةً تليها أخرى فأخرى وملفات الأمن والبنية التحتية تراوح فى مكانها ،الشعب الليبى طيب ومطالبه بسيطة وتُعدّ حقوقًا أساسية ، على الشعب واجب دعم الحكومة ولكن على الحكومة الاهتمام بشعبها فالمواطن الذى لا يجد قوت يومه سيخرج يومًا شاهرًا سيفه وعندها من يلومه . مسئولية إعادة إعمار ليبيا تقع على أعتاقنا جميعًا وعلى كل منّا أمانة إصلاح نفسه وأهله وبيته

رحلة الأمل والشفاء

وفّقنى الله عام 2006 أن استقبل رسالة الكترونيه عن طريق الصدفة من جامعة هارفارد أكبر جامعات أمريكا أنهم بصدد إقامة برنامج ماجستير طب نفسى للاجئين والناجين من الحروب والكوارث، اتصّلت بهم وكونى العربى والمسلم الوحيد الذى قدّم تلك السنه وكون تركيزهم كان على الشرق الأوسط خصوصًا بعد حرب العراق فقد وافقوا على إعطائى الفرصة دون مقابل وحسنًا فعلت باشتراكى فما تعلمته من تلك التجربة ساعدنى كثيرًا أن أخدم ناسى وأهلى خلال الحرب على ليبيا

طبيب نفسى

منذ صغرى كنت أعلم أنى أريد أن أكون طبيبًا، أختى زكيّه التى أصطفاها الله إلى جواره وهى أبنة أربعة عشر عامًا والتى أنقذت حياتى مرَّة من صعق كهربائى، أختى الحبيبه فقدت بصرها بسبب ورم فى الدماغ و انتقلت إلى رحمة الله يوم اعلان نتيجة امتحانها النهائى وجاءت معلمتها تبكى وتعلن أن الفقيدة العمياء قد نجحت بتفوّق، رغم كونى فى السادسة من عمرى حينها ولم أفهم تمامًا معنى الموت ولا دموع أمَّى كنت أعى أن السرطان شىء خبيث وقرّرت حينها أن أتخصص طبيبًا أعالج أمراض الرأس وقد مَنّ الله علىّ بدخول كليّة الطب والعمل كطبيب إسعاف وطوارئ لكنى كنت منجذبًا للمعاناة الشخصية والنفسية والعائلية لمن هو أمامى وكنت أراه كإنسانٍ لا مجرّد أعراض ولا أنسى أنّنى قضيت قرابة الساعة مع أحد المرضى الذى كان يعانى من أعراضٍ جسمانية شخّصتها كقلقٍ ونصحته بأجازة من عمله المرهق فنظر إلىّ طويلاً وقال أنه يرانى طبيبًا نفسانيا ويرانى قد خرجت للتخصّص خارج البلاد، ضحكت حينها وشكرته فكلاهما لم يكن يخطر لى على بال

الهجرة أمر صادم ولازلت أناقش إخوتى الذين يقولون أننى محظوظ بخروجى من ليبيا وأنا أقول أنهم هم المحظوظون بوجودهم عند قدمى أمى وأبى، فالهجرة تفكك شبكة العلاقات والروابط الاجتماعية وتؤدى إلى الشعور بالعزله والوحدة والكآبة، والعيش بعيدًا عن وطن قد لا تسكنه لكنه يسكن كله خليةٍ فيك أمر ليس باليسير

رحلة الأمل والشفاء

بعضهم عن حمله لابنه الميّت بين يديه وحكى البعض عن رؤية أشلاء زملاء له كان منذ لحظات يشاطرهم حلو العيش ومرّه، البعض حكى قصصًا مؤلمه لكن دون مشاعر وكأنما يقرأ قصّه أو يحكى عن واقع لم يعايشه، البعض التجأ إلى العمل بكثرة أو السفر أو غيرها من وسائل التجنّب، البعض حكى عن أشباح تطارده في نومه وتقض مضجعه والبعض حكى عن خلافات عائليه فلم يعد للجلوس بجانب الزوجة أو الأسرة معنى بعد فقد الأصحاب، أحد الثوار فقد تمامًا شهيته ثم حاسّة الشمّ كونه اشتم رائحة لحم زملائه وقد أحرقتهم القذائف. كان لى شرفٌ مشاركتهم تلك اللحظات الخاصة ومشاطرتهم مشاعرهم وذكرياتهم فبارك الله فيهم أن فتحوا لى بيوتهم وقلوبهم. لاحظت كذلك أن البعض لا يريد إعطاء نفسه الإذن حتى بمساحة صغيرة من الفرح -أفرحُ بليبيا أولاً ثم بنفسى، لكن أليس أن نهتم بأنفسنا ونفرح ونُشفى معًا جزء كبير من شفاء ليبيا وفرحها

رحلة الأمل والشفاء

السبورة كان كافيًا لرؤية كبر الجرح واتساع الخرق وأن كل يد تستطيع البناء أو تقديم شيء يجب احترامها وإعطائها الفرصة وأنّ الآن وقت الاتحاد والعمل ونبذ الخلاف والفرقه. وسبحانِ القائل –وأطيعوا الله ورسوله ولاتنازعوا فتفشلوا وتذهب ريحكم واصبروا إن الله مع الصابرين

نصائح فعَّاله جرّبتها خلال الحرب كان من ضمّنها

.لاتقارن نفسك بالآخرين

لاتجعل الآخرين يحدّدون أهدافك

لاتضيع الحاضر بالعيش في الماضي أو المستقبل

لا تطلب الكمال لكن دومًا إسعَ للتحسين

أسرع طريقة لتلقّى الحب أو الاحترام هي إعطاؤه

إصنع أحلامًا وأهدافًا لكن بواقعيه

لا تجرى خلال الحياة بسرعة تنسيك من أين بدأت وإلى أين أنت ذاهب

الحياة ليست سباقًا بل رحله، تلذّذ بكل خطوه ومحطّه فيها

التخطيط والتنظيم أمور مهّمه لضبط الوقت والنجاح

ساعد الآخرين ولكن بحدود، تعلّم قول لا أحيانًا، واهتّم بنفسك أولاً

ومن أجمل التجارب التي خضتها حلقات الدعم للثوار الذين كان البعض منهم قد تحول إلى شخص طويل الصمت قليل الكلام والابتسام خصوصًا عند الحديث عن رفاقهم الذين قضوا أو عن اليتامى والأرامل الذين خلفتهم الحرب، حكى

رحلة الأمل والشفاء

كثير من الليبيين مصاب بخيبة الأمل والأحباط بسبب عدم إحراز تطوّرات ملحوظة فى مجالات عدّه. وأنا بالرغم من كونى من أشدّ الناس تفاؤلاً وثقة بربى إلا أننى أحيانًا تعترينى غصة فى الحلق وحرقة فى القلب من كثرة السلبيات التى انتشرت فى البلاد. وقد لاحظت أيضًا سواءً فى داخل ليبيا أو خارجها أن المعانى الجميلة التى كانت تجمع الناس فى أول الثورة كالترابط والتآخى والتضحية والإيثار أصبحت تقلّ وهذا من المحزن فعلينا من أجل احترام دماء الشهداء أن نحقق ما ماتوا فى سبيله، وقد قيل أن الأمانه يوم القيامة خزى وندامه إلا من أخذها بحقّها واتقى الله فيها فلا أعلم لماذا يتقاتل الإخوه من أجل كراسى وسلطة تزول ولا تدوم. ورغم كل الألم يظل الأمل مشتعلاً ومنيرًا فليس مع الصبر إلا النصر ولا بعد العسر إلا اليسر وكلما ضاقت انفرجت وكلما اشتد الكرب اقترب الفرج، ومما يعطينى شرحًا فى الصدر جنود مجهولون يقومون بأعمال يستحقون الوقوف لها احترامًا من تنظيم وتنظيف للبلاد لاينتظرون مناصب ولا رواتب ولاشهرة بل يعملونها خالصة لوجه الله وحبًا لليبيا، ورغم أن كثيرًا من الشباب يود الخروج من البلاد إما هجرةً أو دراسة أو تنفيسًا إلا أننى أجزم أن حبّ ليبيا أقوى فى قلوب أبنائها من خيبات الأمل المتكررة

من الأشياء التى حزّت فى نفسى ولازالت تثير استغرابى وجود حساسيات بين فرق الدعم النفسى والاجتماعى وكأنما البعض يرى ليبيا كبقرة حلوب لا كأم رؤوم وقد رأيت البعض يطالب الناس بأن يطلقوا عليه لقب دكتور وهو لم يتحصل حتى على الماجستير ورأيت البعض يخفى فوائد ومشاريع تنفع غيره لحاجة فى نفسه وعند سؤالى قيل لى بأنه لا توجد سوق لكل المتخصّصين وكأنما لم نعلم بأن الخالق هو نفسه الرازق والنظر إلى الجراح الليبية كسوق أو غنيمه أمر أراه مقرفاً. لمّا اجتمعت ببعضهم وتطرّقت إلى أن الدعم النفسى سيشمل أطفال الشهداء وأطفال الكتائب وزوجات الشهداء والكتائب وأمهات وأخوات وبنات وعائلات هؤلاء وأولئك وكذلك الأسرى من الطرفين والمخطوفين والمفقودين والراجعين من الجبهات ومبتورى الأطراف ومرضى ما قبل الحرب والمعاقين وذوى الاحتياجات الخاصة والفتن بين القبائل والمدن والمناطق ودور الرعاية والإصلاح ومؤسسات الدولة والمجتمع المدنى والمدارس والمستشفيات والمتطوعين كالكشافة والهلال الأحمر والأخصائيين المجروحين أنفسهم وضحايا النزوح والاغتصاب ودورنا فى تطوير المناهج والتنمية البشرية وبناء الإنسان، لمّا ذكرت ذلك كله وكتبته على

ما بعد الفتح

يقول سبحانه - لايستوى منكم من أنفق من قبل الفتح وقاتل أولئك أعظم درجةً من الذين أنفقوا من بعد وقاتلوا وكلاً وعد الله الحسنى والله بما تعملون خبير. لايراودنى شك فى أنه ليس الثائر الصادق كالمفترى وليس الرجال كأشباههم وشتّان ما بين الثرى والثريّا

للأسف بمجرد تحرير البلاد ترك البعض ما كان عليه من صلاح والتزام واتجّه إلى تطبيق مفهومه للحريّه فمن مُطالب بالعلمانية إلى مُجاهر بالمعاصى مُحارب للسُنّه ومن مخالف للقوانين غير معترف بشرعية الحكومات المنتخبه بعد القذافى إلى مُطالب بدس السم فى الدسم برفع شعارات تحرير المرأة والحرية الجنسية والتخلص من العادات والتقاليد الجميلة للمجتمع المسلم المحافظ الذى حباه الله بأن تكون ليبيا بالكامل دولة مسلمة سنّيّه فيها يتعايش الإخوه متحابّين ومن أراد العيش معهم من أقليات دينية أو عرقيه محترمون، فلماذا تطفو على السطح الآن شعارات زرع الفتن والشقاق ولماذا التنابز بالألقاب فمن خرج مضطرًا من مدينته خائفًا على شرف أهله قد مُنع أحيانًا من الرجوع إليها ووصف بأنه من العائدين الغير مُرحّب بهم، ولماذا يتحمّل طفل وزر أبيه، لماذا يوصف البعض بالعماله والموالاه من غير دليل، ولماذا تحصل حالات قبض واختطاف واغتيال وانتهاكات لحقوق الإنسان من تعذيب وتجريم وتخوين، ولماذا أصبح تعاطى الخمر والمسكرات من حشيش ومخدرات أمراً طبيعيًا ومنظرًا اعتياديًا فى شوارع بلدى، ولماذا تخاف أختى أن تمشى فى الشارع لتربّص الذئاب البشرية بها يعاكسونها بأبذأ الألفاظ، ولماذا ولماذا توقفت أصوات التكبير فى مآذن بلدى وأصبح الرقص والغناء والاختلاط بدائل للذكر والاستغفار والدعاء سلاح المؤمن

رحلة الأمل والشفاء

الاقتراح الذى أقدّمه للمصالحة مبنّى على اقتراحات

2002 Prendergast and Plumb

وهو مشروع مكون من ثمان خطوات متوازية ومكمّله لبعضها

الاهتمام بالصحة النفسية واحتياجاتها فى أفراد المجتمع المتضرر من العنف

عمل حلقات نقاش لمناقشة المشاكل وحلّها

إيجاد وسائل سلميّه لفض النزاع

دور الإعلام وأهميته للتقليل من الإشاعة ولنشر الوعى الصحى ورسائل التسامح

تكوين لجِان سلام مهمّتها تحديد كيفية القصاص على أساس العدل

الاهتمام بوسائل الاستشفاء المحلّيه

تشجيع الأنشطة التى تجمع أفراد المجتمع- خصوصًا من طرفى النزاع – وهنا يأتى دور أنشطة الأطفال والنساء ومؤسسات المجتمع المدنى

تعزيز حقوق الإنسان ومعانى العدل والمساواة

النزاعات المسلّحة تسبّب شروخًا عميقة بين الطرفين المتصارعين وتزرع الشك وعدم الثقة، وضاعف ذلك فى الحالة الليبيّه التهجير و حالات الثأر الفرديّه وجميعنا يعلم أن الشعور بالسلامة والأمن والانتماء عناصر مهمه للصحة النفسية وسلامتها

رحلة الأمل والشفاء

الله فى آيه واحده -خذ العفو وأمر بالعُرف وأعرض عن الجاهلين
نحن نعلم من التجربة أن الإنسان إذا أحس بالخطر نكص فى المرحلة العمرية فالطفل قد يتبوّل على نفسه أو يقضم أظافره والبالغ قد يتضايق أو يغضب بسهولة وبالمثل فالمجتمع ينطوى على نفسه ويصبح الولاء للقبيلة أو الطائفة أو المذهب رغم أن الكل كان ينادى بوحدة ليبيا حينما كان الهدف واضحا . وقد زاد الطين بلّة فى ليبيا ما حذّرنا منه منذ البداية أن الكثير من المنظمات الدولية لحاجة فى نفسها حاولت فرض برامج ترى هى أنها مفيدة دون أخذ فى الاعتبارات لخصوصيات القضيّة الليبية مما أدى إلى فشل تلك البرامج التى رأى المستهدفون منها أنها غريبة بل مُريبه فكان الكثير منها مضيعةً للوقت والمال والله المستعان كما أسلفت فإنّ إعادة التعمير وبناء مؤسسات الدولة وتكوين الجيش

والانتخابات كلها أمور حسنه لكنها لاتعنى شيئًا إذا أهملنا الإنسان الذى يسير نازفًا ، لابد له من الإحساس بكرامته وقيمته وأهمية تضحيته ومعاناته ، فالكل فى ليبيا تأثر بالحرب وعزاؤنا واحد فلا عيب ولاحرام أن نضع أيدينا معنا ونبكى ونُشفَى معًا . مشاعر الغضب والكراهية هى الشائعة الآن فى ليبيا فيجب أن نتوقف عن وصف الماء الذى يكاد يغمرنا وعلينا بدل ذلك البحث عن أطواق النجاة

فى ظل الحقد والعزله فإننا نتوقف عن رؤية الآخر كإنسان بل قد نراه هدفًا لرصاصنا أو كبش فداء لثاراتنا . ومن المهم جدًا هنا التذكير أن المصالحة لا تعنى المسامحة أو النسيان ، بل العكس تعنى أن نعترف بأن آلامًا كثيرة وجرائم فظيعه حصلت لكن لا نعطيها الحق أن تشلّنا ، فمن أقل واجبنا على شهدائنا احترام ما ضحوا من أجله وذلك بالمضى قدمًا وخلق غد أفضل ومستقبل أجمل لأولادهم . التعايش السطحى بين الجيران أو ادّعاء أن كلّ شىء مايرام وسائل بدائية تضر أكثر مما تنفع ، ولابد بدلا منها من جلسات المصارحة والاعتراف وطلب الصفح والقصاص

من الوسائل الناجحة والتى تم تطبيقها فى مجتمعات كان المشهد فيها شبيهًا بليبيا كبوسنيا ورواندا وجنوب أفريقيا أن يُسمَع من طرفى النزاع أو الصراع، ثم إن تم الاتفاق فالجلوس على طاولة الحوار من أجل طرح أفكار لحل المشاكل القائمة والاشتراك فى مشاريع شفاء طويلة الأمد

لقصاص أم المصالحة

محاولات كثيرة من أجل تحقيق العدالة والمصالحة تم اقتراحها، لكن الجرح الليبى لن يتم شفاؤه إلا بأيد ليبيّة ولابد من أجل أن يتوقف العنف ويعم الأمن والسلام وأن لا تنتشر عدوى الكراهية بين الأجيال والتى قد تزعزع مستقبل ليبيا لوقتٍ طويل، لابد من خطوات جادّه من أناس تحب هذا البلد الطيب ولاتخشى فى الله لومة لائم. علّمنا التاريخ أن الحلول من جانب واحد حلول تلفيقية وأن الشعارات التى يرفعها البعض كالتعويض المادى والبناء الحسى هى جوفاء مالم يقابلها شفاء معنوى وبناء للإنسان. أنا لا أقلّل من أهميّة العمران المادى فى شفاء الجرح الليبى لكن ذلك وحده لايكفى، أنا أقترح التركيز على إيجاد حلول جادّه مستعجله طويلة الأمد للأفراد والمجتمعات التى تعرّضت للعنف وذلك بدعم البرامج المحلّية وفتح جسور للحوار وفض النزاع بطرق سلميّه وهذا قد يستغرق وقتًا طويلاً لكنه أفضل من دس الرؤوس فى الرمال وادعاء أن الجراح لا تنزف، والحلول الواهنة التى ستضر أكثر ممّا تنفع. لابد أولاً من دعوة أفراد المجتمع المتضرّرين من العنف لمناقشة شؤونهم والمشاكل التى تواجهم والحلول المقترحة لها وتذليل العراقيل فى وجه تلك الحلول، فبمجرد إشراك الشخص فى مناقشة مشكلته ووسائل حلها هى رسالة بأنه شخص فعّال ومهم فى المجتمع وأن ما حدث لم يحطّمه فالضربة التى لاتكسر ظهرك تقوّيه والأفضل التعلّم من الماضى وعدم حبس النفس فيه، بل تقبّلُه بخيره وشرّه من أجل واقع ومستقبل أفضل.

وكذلك فأنه لا يحس بحرارة النار إلا من كان يطؤها بقدمه، فالمجتمع المحلّى هو الأدرى بشؤونه وظروفه وعاداته وتقاليده التى لابد من احترامها حتى إن لم نتفق معها ثم إن شرائح المجتمع المتعددة مهمّه فى عملية الشفاء فليس فقط الطبيب فى مستشفاه بل المدرّس فى مدرسته والإمام فى مسجده والأم فى بيتها الكل يساهم بما يقدر فى تقديم النصح وبذل الخير، وللّه درّ من قال أن المعاملات بين الناس جمعها

رحلة الأمل والشفاء

لا بأس من استمرار العمل التطوعي في المرحلة الراهنة الحرجة لكن يجب أن

تتحمل الدولة مسئوليتها بتعيين المختصين على حسب الكادر الوظيفي ورفع الرواتب وأعطاء الحوافز خاصة للراغبين في العمل في مناطق نائيه
فتح خط ساخن للراغبين في مناقشة مشاكل بصورة سرّية

العلاجات المحلية الصحيحة وزيادة الشبكات الاجتماعية من أهم وسائل تسريع عملية الشفاء

أهمية التنسيق والتعاون وتبادل الخبرات والنتائج بين الفرق المحلّية للإفادة ومنع التكرار المؤدي إلى الإحباط وعدم الثقة وينطبق نفس الكلام على مؤسسات الدولة والمنظمات الدولية

إعادة النظر في المناهج المحلّية الحالية لضمان استمرار قوة الجانب النظري لكن مع التركيز على الجانب العملي التطبيقي ، كذلك فتح مكتبات الكترونية واعطاء الفرص للخريجين لحضور دورات لغة وحاسوب وتنميه بشريه ومؤتمرات في الداخل والخارج

محاولة الوصول للطلبة الراغبين في دخول مجالات طب وعلم النفس والاجتماع للتأكد من صدق رغبتهم وتوافر معايير الشخصية المتزنة فيهم

توفير الاختبارات النفسية ذات المصداقية ودورات التدريب عليها وتطبيقها ، وتشجيع مجالات البحث في علوم النفس والاجتماع عن طريق مؤسسات أكاديمية ، وتشجيع التخصصات الدقيقة مع التعاون فيما بينها

إنشاء قواعد توثيق بيانات ودراسات ميدانية في المجالات البحثية والإكلينيكية

رحلة الأمل والشفاء

التعاون الأكاديمي وتبادل الخبرات مع جامعات عالمية عالية المستوى
توحيد الجهود ولمّ الشمل بين الفرق العاملة حاليًا فى ليبيا لزيادة تأثير البرامج المقدَّمة واختيار الأكفاء للقيادة وإنهاء استبداد الأفراد من غير ذوى الكفاءة
تكليف أخصائيّين فى مختلف الوزارات والمؤسسات التعليمية والمستشفيات

ومراكز إعادة التأهيل والمعسكرات ودور الرعاية وغيرها
توعية المسئولين بأهمية دور الأخصائى النفسى والاجتماعى فى إعادة تأهيل المجتمع ككل وخاصة توعيه أفراد الأمن والقضاء لحماية المريض النفسى فى مؤسسات الإصلاح

توعية الطواقم الطبيّة بأهمية العامل النفسى فى تسريع عملية الشفاء
إعداد وتطبيق برامج واقعية لإعادة التأهيل النفسى والاجتماعى ولعملية المصالحة
لايجوز لمختص النفس والاجتماع الاشتراك فى عمليات التعذيب أو استغلال الآخرين ماديًا أو جسديًا أو عاطفيًا أو بأى وسيلة استغلال أخرى

إنشاء مراكز إيواء فى المستشفيات العامة وفى أغلب المدن الليبية لتحسين مستوى الخدمات والحد من المركزية

الاهتمام بمشاكل الإدمان والتوحّد والتأخّر الذهنى والناجين من التعذيب والعنف الجسدى والتركيز على شريحة الأطفال مع محاولة دمج ذوى الاحتياجات الخاصة فى المدارس والمؤسسات العامة

فتح مراكز استشفاء نهارية لمتابعة الحالات بعد الخروج من المستشفى وكذلك تكوين فرق للمتابعة والزيارة الميدانية للعلاج النفسى الأسرى والبيئى
الاهتمام بالعلاج باللعب والفن والقصة والرواية وتشجيع الأنشطة الترفيهية والتربوية فى المدارس وكذلك توفير وانشاء حدائق ومراكز تنفيس بالتعاون مع الكشافة والهلال الأحمر ومؤسسات المجتمع المدنى

لا بأس من الاستفادة من خبرات المنظمات الدولية والتعاون معها لكن ببرامج وطواقم ليبية تحترم ديننا وثقافتنا وعاداتنا وتقاليدنا وطريقة تفكيرنا

لرحله الرابعة

أكرمنى الله بأن أعود مرّه رابعه إلى ليبيا فى يونيو عام 2012، هذه المرّة معى زوجتى وبناتى، منظمة هلفزورك النمساوية اختارتنى كمستشارها النفسى والاجتماعى من أجل الإشراف على تدريب الأخصائيين النفسيين وتقييم أداء المركز الليبى للشباب فى طرابلس

هذا وقد تم بحمد الله وفضله وتوفيقه، إقامة المؤتمر الأول للصحة النفسية فى ليبيا الحرّة برئاستى فى مدينة مصراته وكان الحضور طيّباً من مختلف مدن ليبيا الحبيبة وتوصّل إلى التوصيات التالية للرفع من مستوى الخدمات النفسية والاجتماعيه

نشر الوعى والثقافة النفسية والاجتماعية للمواطن الليبى عن طريق وسائل الاتصالات المختلفة كالتلفاز والراديو والانترنت والمطويات والنشرات وورش العمل والمحاضرات وغيرها

رفع درجة الوعى النفسى والاجتماعى لأئمة المساجد والدعاة والمعالجين بالرقية الشرعية الصحيحة وتصحيح مفاهيم علم النفس الإسلامى

فريق الصحة النفسية المثالى يعمل كفريق ويتكون من أخصائى نفسى وطبيب نفسى وممرض نفسى وأخصائى اجتماعى، كحد أدنى

الارتقاء بأخلاقيات المهنة إلى مستوى المعايير العالمية عن طريق إنشاء نقابات للتدريب والرقابة والمتابعة الهدف منها رفع كفاءة العناصر الليبية لضمان عدم استمرار الممارسات الخاطئة كمزاولة المهنة دون خبرة أو وصف عقاقير من غير الأطباء أو ادعاء امتلاك درجة أو شهادة علميه

التعاون مع وزارات الدولة من أجل بدء برامج ماجستير ودكتوراه وزماله ليبّيه رفيعة المستوى

رحلة الأمل والشفاء

غاليه يجب الحفاظ عليها وتقدير التضحيات والدماء التى سُكبت من أجلها، رأى آخرون أن لا فرق بين الحرية والفوضى فأصبح عدم احترام إشارات المرور وإطلاق الرصاص العشوائى والقيادة المتهورة والتحرّش بالنساء وعمليات التصفية والانتقام الفردية حوادث نسمع بها من حين لآخر للأسف. وصحيح أن هناك أيد خفيّه لا تريد لليبيا الخير ولا الاستقرار إلا أننى مؤمن أن على كل منّا مسئوليه وأن كل واحد منا جندى على باب من أبواب الإسلام فلا أقل من أن لا يحصل الغدر من تلك الناحية، صحيح أن البيت الليبى مهّدم بالكامل لكن لو نظّف كل منّا المساحة التى أمامه ستنظف وتترتب البلاد كلها

الرحلة الثالثه

ذهبت مجدّداً إلى ليبيا فى منتصف ديسمبر عام 2011 للعمل على برنامج ليبيا الشفاء، كانت قضية المصالحة الوطنية تطغى على الساحة بعد مقتل القذافى لكن لابد من أشياء كثيره قبل المصالحة منها

سن قوانين وتشريعات عن طريق حكومة منتخَبة للحد من الثأر والقتل اللامشروع تطبيق العدالة فى حدودها ومن قِبل القضاء النزيه خصوصاً فى مسائل الدم والاغتصاب

دور المؤسسات الغير حكوميه والجمعيات الخيرية مهم وينبغى تفعيله رفع مستوى المعيشة من جميع نواحيها المادية والمعنويه والنفسيه والحرفيه وغيرها

إحقاق الحق هو الخطوة الأولى فى طريق السلام والصفح
رفع درجة وعى الشارع الليبى بآثار الحرب السلبية على البناء النفسى والاجتماعى

برامج دعم واستشفاء لجراح الحرب النفسية كالحِداد، سواء كان الدعم فردياً أو فى مجموعات

فض النزاعات بطرق سلميه غير مسلّحه

عمل برامج مجتمعيه كالخيمه الرمضانية لفتح أبواب التواصل والتعاون

الدعم المادى لهذه الأنشطة مهم من أجل استمرارها

الحرية فى ليبيا أصبح لها معنىً آخر عند البعض. ففى حين أن أغلبنا اعتبرها سلعه

رحلة الأمل والشفاء

ماذا كان عسي ان يفعل، أصبح يحكي أثناء نومه لأول مرّه، وأحياناً يقوم فزعاً يتصبّب عرقاً، كان يتسلّل لينام في غرفة أخرى خشية إيقاظى أو طفلتنا ولم يدر أننى كنت صاحيه خوفاً أن يحتاجني مرّةً فلا يجدني. زوجى الذى غادر إلى ليبيا ليس نفس الشخص الذى عاد منها، حمل آلام الملايين على ظهره وشاب شعره بسرعه، الشعور بالذنب وتأنيب الضمير أرّق نومه ونغّص أكله ومنعه من التركيز على عمله، أصبح قليل الكلام والابتسام، كان بصره متعلقًا بالتلفاز عسى يسمع أخباراً سارّة. الحرب التي اشتعلت في ليبيا اشتعلت كذلك في قلبه وعقله، وعرفت أنه لن يهدأ حتى تنتهى الحرب وأنه سيعود مرّات ومرّات. كان مجروحاً ومتألماً لكن لم يُرد أن يشاركه أحد همّه. أخبرنى أنه لابد له من الذهاب إلى مصراته في شدة وقت حصارها، هذه المرة لم أبكِ بل بالعكس التجأت للصلاة والدعاء وطلبت من الله العون والاستخارة، سألت الله له راحة البال وأن يرجع لى زوجى كما كان قبل الحرب. كانت ستة أشهر قضيتها في الجحيم لكن بقربي من الله كنت دوماً أرى بصيصًا من نور وأمل في نهاية النفق

ركّزت على أن أعشق كل لحظة لنا معًا وأتعامل معها كأنها الأخيرة، ماذا كان عساي أن أفعل، بل ماذا كان عساه

رحلة الأمل والشفاء

أغرقت الوسادة بدموعي، حاول هو إسكاتي لكن دموعه كانت أثقل. كنت غاضبه منه، غاضبه من فكرة رحيله، لكن إن لم أوافق فلن أسامح نفسي وربما هو أبداً لن يسامحني. حاول أهلي إثنائه عن عزمه لكن من غير فائده، قرّرت السفر إلى أهلي فلا سمح الله إن حصل أي شئ له كنت أريد أن تحاط البنات بحنان أهلي. لا زلت أذكر غضبى من غلاء سعر التذاكر وكيف أوقفت السيارة في المكان الخطأ في موقف المدرسة وكيف فرحت البنات بالسفر إلى بيت جدّتهن. أمسك هو يدي ونظر في عيني وأخبرني بكل هدوء كعادته أن كل شئ سيكون على ما يرام، لكن لم يكن بإمكاني تصديق ذلك هذه المرّة. هذا أكبر حدث مسّ حياتنا حتى اليوم وقد يكون الأخير وحتى إن عاد عُمر فكل شئ لن يكون كما قبل، هذا الحدث سيغير حياتنا للأبد

ودّعته في المطار، لم أُرد أن أترك يده، اتصّل بي من الطائرة وترك لي رسالةً صوتيه لا زلت أحتفظ بها حتى اليوم، كنت استمع إليها كل ليله وكانت أمى تخبرني أنني أصرخ وأتقلّب طوال الليل، هل أُصبتُ بالجنون

للمرة الأولى في حياتي أدركت حقيقة صعوبة الفراق، ليبيا كانت منطقة حرب خطيره وغير تقليديّه. رُغم أنه وعدني أنه سيعود لكنّ خِفت أن يبقى في ليبيا فالبلد تحتاجه فهو طبيب نفسي متخصص في طب الحروب والكوارث وخلفيته في ليبيا كطبيب طوارئ تجعله في موضع أن يقدّم الكثير من العون

كنت أنتظر أن يتّصل بي من مصر، مرّت الساعات كالسنين وأخيراً اتّصل، ثم مرّت أيام قبل وصوله إلى بنغازي، كان يحاول مكالمتي عن طريق هاتف خلوي من فوق سطح بنايه، توسلت إليه أن ينزل فلربما كان هناك قنّاصه، كان صوته سعيداً جدّاً، أخبرني أنه يشم رائحة الحرّية وأن الحرب ستنتهى عن قريب، كم كان مخطئاً. اتصلت بوالده ورجوته أن يقنع عمر بالعوده، وعدني أنه سيفعل وبعد ثلاثة أسابيع رجع عمر شخصاً مختلفاً، كان جسده هنا وقلبه هناك، المناظر التي شاهدها ستعيش معه إلى الأبد. أخبرني أنه كان يخبئ سكيناً تحت مخدّته في حال اقتحمت الكتائب بيتهم، ماذا كان عسى السكين أن يفعل

ما بين نارين

هذا ما كتبته زوجتى نورا عندما كنت فى ليبيا، لازلت لا أتمالك نفسى من البكاء كلّما قرأت رسالتها، عُذرى أنها والبنات كُنّ مع أصهارى وبأمان بينما أطفال ليبيا يُقتَلون ويتَيتّمون فلا أقل من أن أضحى ببعض وقتى وعلمى من أجلهم عندما أخبرنى أنه قرّر الذهاب لم أدر ماذا أقول أو أفعل أو حتى أشعر، لماذا؟ كررت السؤال مراراً فى رأسى. المرة الأولى التى ذهب فيها عمر لليبيا كان فقط يُردّد «يجب علىّ أن أساعد»، تلك كانت أسوأ أيام، خلال الأسبوع الأول من الحرب، أن تسمع صوت أحبائك على التليفون يودّعونك بقولهم أن الملتقى فى الجنّة، أن أرى زوجى يبكى لمجرد تفكيره بأن عائلته ومدينته وبلاده على وشك أن تُباد، ليس بالأمر السهل ولا اليسير. بالنسبه لى كنت أتألم من أجل ليبيا لكن ليس كعُمر فأهله هناك بينما أنا أهلى هنا، كبرت وتربيّت بعيداً عن بلدى الذى دومًا أحببته. بكيت كل يوم من شدّة انشغالى على بلد عشقته ولم تطأه قدماى. الصور لا زالت عالقة فى ذهنى والذكريات تمّر فى وجدانى. أن ترى شخصاً يموت أمامك أو جسدًا تشطره القذائف نصفين ليس أمراً كنت أتمنى مشاهدته، لكن للأسف أصبح كالأمر المعتاد بل الطبيعى، البعض مات مقاتلاً فى الجبهة مدافعاً عن الحرية بينما البعض ربما كان فى المكان الخاطئ فى التوقيت الخاطئ توسلت إليه أن لا يغادر، بكيت وهدّدته، لم أعن ما أقول حينها، قلت للبنات أن أباكن ذاهب إلى ساحة حرب وقد لا يعود، ماذا كان عساى أن أفعل

حجز تذكرته وتوسّل إلىّ أن أسامحه، شعرت بثقل موافقتى على قلبى، تلك الليلة نمت بين ذراعيه وتعلّقت به بشدّه، لم نعرف إن كانت هذه ليله سنقضيها معاً، هل سنرى بعضنا مرة أخرى أم أننى سأصبح أرمله وأمًا لثلاث طفلات يتيمات سيذكرن أباهن كبطل

رحلة الأمل والشفاء

جسمانيه ككثرة التعرق والهلع وضيق التنفس وزيادة نبضات القلب وفى حالة الأطفال آلام البطن أو تغيّرات المزاج وهذه كلها قد تؤثر على التحصيل المدرسى أو الأداء الوظيفى أو العلاقات الأسرية والاجتماعيه

تعرفت على إخوة وأخوات أفاضل فى جمعيات خيريه وقسّمت وقتى بين عناصر برنامج ليبيا الشفاء السبع

زيادة الوعى النفسى والاجتماعى عن طريق المحاضرات وورش العمل والمطويات وبرامج الراديو والتلفاز

رفع كفاءة الأخصائيين النفسيّين والاجتماعيّين المحليين

عمل برامج علاج باللعب والفن للأطفال
عمل حلقات دعم

عمل حلقات لأسر الشهداء والمعتقلين والمفقودين ومحاولة فتح مراكز استشفاء نهاريّة

العمل على إنشاء خط ساخن للاستشارات السرية كالمتعلقه بالعنف الجسدى والإدمان

تشجيع حل الخلافات بالطرق السلمية وفتح النقاش عن القصاص والمصالحه

رحلة الأمل والشفاء

رأينا تغيّرات فى رسومات الأطفال وطريقة تعبيرهم بمجرد تقديم الدعم النفسى والاجتماعى لهم وتحسنت علاقاتهم بذويهم عن طريق استخدام أساليب العلاج باللعب والفن وجداول تعديل السلوك واستبدال العقاب بالحرمان من الثواب، فالطفل الليبى يكفيه ضرباً وإهانة فهذا عهد جديد نريد فيه بناء الإنسان قوى الشخصية والثقة بالنفس

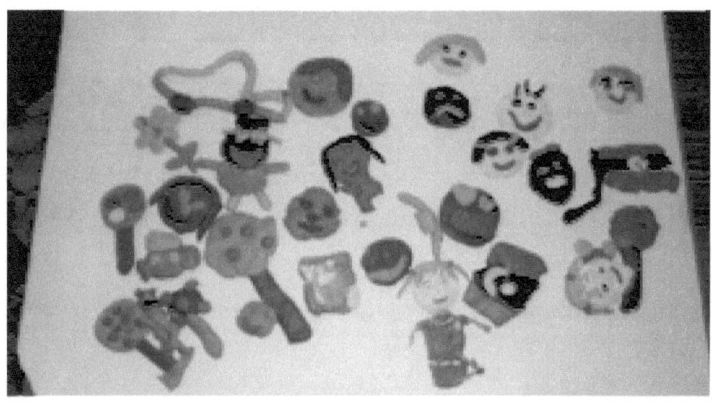

اضطراب كرب ما بعد الصدمة ظاهره معروفه بعد التعرض لحادث صادم قد تؤدى بالشخص إلى تكرار معايشة التجربة عن طريق تكرار مشاهدها فى النوم أو اليقظة مما قد يدفعه إلى تجنّب أى موقف أو مكان يذكّره بالصدمه وقد يرافق ذلك أعراض

رحلة الأمل والشفاء

وأجلس هنا ألعب مع الأطفال وطلبوا منى الذهاب معهم للجبهة، لكنى أخبرتهم أن جبهتى هنا وأنه إن لم يكتب الله لى شرف الشهادة فى جبهة القتال فأساله سبحانه أن لايحرمنى أجرها فى ساحة العناية باليتامى والأرامل

الجمعيات الخيريَّة المحليَّة قامت أيضًا بمجهودات رائعه كان لى شرف الاشتراك فى بعض مناشطهم ورأيت كيف كان التعبير بالرسم والفن والشعر والدراما وغيرها يُساعد الطفل فى التعامل مع آثار الحرب البغيضة، فكلنا يعلم أنه لابد للطفل من أجل أن ينمو سليماً ذا شخصية قويّة من أن يشعر أن العالم مكان آمن وأنه يمكنه الثقة بالبالغين، والحرب تشوّش وتشوّه تلك المعانى، فكان لابد من إضافة بعض الروتين وإضفاء بعض طعم الحياة الطبيعية لهؤلاء الأطفال حتى لا يعانوا أعراضاً مزمنة. وفى الحقيقة أنى تعلّمت من الأطفال أكثر ممّا علّمتهم وهم دخلوا قلبى وغيّروا حياتى إلى الأبد ولهم الفضل أنى كإنسان وكطبيب أفضل

الرحلة الثانية

بعد رجوعى إلى الولايات المتحدة تواصلت مع إخوة أفاضل من أطباء الخارج الذين كانت تملؤهم الوطنية والحماس ولكن ينقصهم بعض التنظيم والدعم. وكان من فيالق الرحمة التى كانت Mercy Corps حسن حظى أن اتصلت بى منظمة بصدد الشروع فى برامج دعم نفسى واجتماعى لأطفال مصراته، وحسنًا فعلت ففى رحلتى وجدت معنى حياتى وشعرت بحلاوة وقيمة ما أنا مُقدم عليه

الجزء المُحبّب إلى قلبى فى عملى فى مصراته كانت ليالى رمضان، فقد أقمنا برنامج خيمة الدعم النفسى والاجتماعى فى ميدان التحرير بوسط المدينة ، وهنا لا أنسى فضل إخوتى وأخواتى الذين تطوعوا لمساعدتى رغم خطورة الموقف وصعوبته فجعل الله كل ما قدّموا فى ميزان حسناتهم. عملنا أنشطة دعم وعلاج باللعب والفن للأطفال وبرامج توعويه واستشارية لأولياء الأمور الذين طلبوا كيفية التعامل مع أعراض الحرب عند الأطفال كالكوابيس والعصبية الزائدة والتأتأه والتبوّل اللاإرادى وما يسمّى بالسلوك العدوانى وغيرها، وكما نعلم فأن الأطفال فى ليبيا قد شاهدوا أشياء ليست مناسبه لا لإعمارهم ولا لأفكارهم والبعض لِصغر سِنّه قد لا يستطيع التعبير عنها بالكلام فيعبّر بالتصرفات ممّا قد يؤدى إلى سوء فهم أو مشاكل فى البيت أو المدرسة. كان البرنامج بفضل الله ناجحًا جدًا وطُلب منا أن نقيم برامج أخرى ولجميع الفئات العُمرية، كانت هذه أجمل تجربة فى حياتى حيث أكرمنى الله بتطبيق ما تعلّمته على مدى السنين الماضية لأساعد أهلى وناسى

من الطرائف التى حصلت أننى كنت أتلفّت كلما سمعت صوت رصاص أو انفجارات لكن الأطفال الذين شبّوا قبل الأوان أخبرونى أنه لاينبغى علىّ الانبطاح إلا فى حالة سماع صواريخ سكود. وكذلك عند رجوع مجموعة من الثوّار من الجبهة أتوا إلى الخيمة وأخبرونى أنه من العيب علىّ أن أكون فى سن القتال

رحلة الأمل والشفاء

والخوف والغضب عن مرضاهم لكن شرّفوني بمشاركتهم إياها ، فمنهم من شرَق بدمعه ومنهم من أبداه وكأنما كان ينتظر إذناً للتعبير عن معاناته فى صمت ، هم أبطالى وكان واجبى أن أعلمهم بأنهم أيضًا بشر لهم مشاعر وأنهم ليسوا وحدهم فكلنا إخوه همّنا واحد وعزاؤنا واحد

لأن الابحاث تدل على أن الإنسان شديد المرونة والمقاومة خاصةً خلال أحداث الحروب فلم أفاجأ بأن التركيز كان على الجروح الظاهرة وعلى الآثار النازفة ، لكن بحكم خبرتى فإنّه كان لزامًا علىّ التذكير بالآثار النفسية والاجتماعية للحروب والجراح الغير مرئيه والتى قد تأخذ وقتًا أطول للتعافى والإلتئام ، البلد كلها كانت فى مرحلة حداد ، عدد الشهداء والجرحى والمفقودين كان فى الآلاف ، عند رؤيتى للأيتام والأرامل وضحايا العنف الجسدى والاغتصاب والتعذيب علمتُ يقينًا أن الأسابيع والشهور القادمة تُحتّم علىّ السفر إلى بلدى تكرارًا ومحاولة الاستقرار بها نهائيًا لأنها ليبيا أمّى وهى الآن تحتاجنى ولا أستطيع أن أقول لا . الشىء الوحيد الذى استطعت أن أعد زوجتى به أن لا أذهب إلى جبهة القتال وأن لا أحمل السلاح إلادفاعا عن النفس ، وقد وفّقنى الله أن ألتزم موعدى رُغم أن الإغراء كان شديدًا

لى الفخر أن استطعت العودة والمساعدة بقدر جُهدى وهذا ليس بطولة منى فأبطالى هم الذين قدموا الغالى والنفيس حتى أرجع أنا إلى بلدى وأرى والدىّ وأهلى فلا أقل من أرد بعضًا من جميلهم بالاعتناء بأسرهم . حاولت قدر الإمكان رفع الوعى النفسى والاجتماعى والتعريف بآثار الحرب وكم كان جميلاً أن أتعرف على المتطوعين فى الجمعيات الخيرية المحلية الذين يقومون بأعمال رائعه قد لا نعلمها لكن الله يعلمهم ويجازيهم عنّا خير الجزاء

بعد عودتى إلى أمريكا لم استطع التركيز على عملى ومرضاى فاستدعانى مديرى وطلب منى الرجوع إلى ليبيا قائلاً لى أن قلبك هناك فأذهب واهتم بأهلك ، وعملك موجود عندما ترجع

الرحلة الأولى

بينما كان العالم يشاهد فى ذهول وعدم تصديق صور القتل والدمار وانتهاك حقوق الإنسان، كنا نحاول أن نوقظ ضمير الإنسانية بإيصال صوتنا عن طريق المظاهرات ووسائل الإعلام. المنظمات الحكومية وغير الحكومية والحقوقية أخبرونا أنهم متضايقون جدًا ويراقبون الأحداث عن كثب، لكنّى وزوجتى نعلم أن القلق والشجب وحده لايكفى وأن تيار الدم لابد أن يتوقف فقد تُمحى مدن من الخارطة قبل أن يتّخذ العالم وقفه جدّيه وخطوات عمليه

بعد مكالمتى مع أمّى قررت الطيران فورًا إلى ليبيا، زوجتى وبناتى كن مذعورات، اتصلت بالعديد من المنظمات آملاً فى أن يتم إرسال فريق يمكننى الالتحاق به، أخبرونى بأنه فى Medical Teams International وللّٰه الحمد ففريق حالة ذهابى فسيوفرون لى أدوية ومعدات طبيه بقيمة نصف مليون دولار لحظة دخولى للبيت كاد يُغشى على أمّى، أخواتى وبناتهن صرخن بهستيريه، ابن اختى الذى تركته فى شهره الخامس عشر يستقبلنى الآن شابا يافعًا، أوقات جميلة وذكريات حلوة سُرقت منى، لكن من الآن وصاعدًا ساعشق كل لحظة فى هذا البلد الحبيب الذى أحس بخفّة ونقاء هوائه وبركة أهله برغم ما شاهدوه فالكل متلاحم متعاطف كأسره واحدة ومعانى التضحية والإيثار والفداء عادت وكيف لا وهى شجرةٌ طيبةٌ سُقيت من دم الشهداء

كان الوضع فى المستشفيات سيئًا جدًا وكان الطلبه والمتطوعون يعوضون الممرضين الذين فرّوا إلى بلدانهم بسبب الحرب

رغم ما مررت به الأطقم الطبيه المجاهده سواءً من أطباء الداخل أو إخوتهم الذين رجعوا من الخارج إلا أن الروح المعنوية كانت عاليه والدافع الوطنى والوازع الدينى كان عظيما. جلست مع أطقم طبيّه كُتب عليها أن ترى وتتعامل مع إصابات ومناظر لم تُذكر فى كُتب الجامعة، حاولوا بشجاعة إخفاء مشاعر الإجهاد

رحلة الأمل والشفاء

مقدمة

بسم الله الرحمن الرحيم
الحمد لله والصلاة والسلام على رسول الله

كنا نتساءل هل الصور والمقاطع والقصص التي نعايشها حقيقة أم اشاعه أم حلم جميل أم كابوس طويل، كنت وزوجتي ملتصقين بالتلفاز نبحث في طيات أخباره عن أمل بين ثنايا الألم. كان القتال عنيفًا والقصف مستمرًا والدم متدفقًا على نحو فقدنا فيه الشعور بالزمان والمكان، بناتنا الثلاثة الصغيرات تعلمن أن يعتمدن على أنفسهن وكبرن في يوم وليله فالانتباه مشتت والتركيز فقط على شيء واحد، ليبيا وسلامتها

لم استطع التركيز على عملي، وزوجتي لم تجد الطاقة لأخذ البنات إلى المدرسة. حتى طفلتي ذات العام والنصف كانت تتناول زجاجة الحليب بنفسها، ورغم محاولاتنا منعهم من مشاهدة التلفاز إلا أنهن كن يعرفن أو يشعرن بأن هناك شيئًا كبيرًا وخطيرًا يشغل بال والديهن

كان الوقت مبكرًا جدًا ذاك الصباح وكدت أن أفقد الأمل بعد أسبوع من عدم النوم ولاسماع صوت الأهل، ولكن حدثت معجزة فقد رن هاتف الوالدة وبكيت حين سمعت صوتها بالله يا أم طمّنيني، أخبرتني أن يا صغيري أسرتك ستموت لكن ليبيا لن تموت، قالت لي أحبّك يابنيّ وفخوره بك لكن سألقاك في الجنة وسامحني، كلمات لن أنساها ما حييت ولازالت ترن في أذني وتوقظني من نومي، لم استطع حينها التحكم في دموعي واتجهت إلى الله كي يرشدني بينما سمعت زوجتي تصرخ على الهاتف احموا أنفسكم، أذهبوا إلى المخابئ وتحت الطاولات، ابتعدوا عن النوافذ، قاتلوا حتى النهاية. أخبرت أمي أني أحبها وأن تسامحني هي وأني سأراها وحين أقفلت السماعة أخبرت زوجتي أني ذاهب

رحلة الأمل والشفاء

شكر وتقدير

ناشطة حقوق الإنسان الأمريكية أماندا لوبيت

رحلة الأمل والشفاء

رحلة الأمل

قصّتى عن الثورة الليبيّة
د- عمر أحمد الرضا
مستشار الطب النفسى -الولايات المتحدة الأمريكية
مؤسس ورئيس مشروع ليبيا الشفاء للدعم النفسى والاجتماعى
مستشار عيادة النفس المطمئنّة

رحلة الأمل والشفاء

د. عمر أحمد الرضا

مستشار الطب النفسي - الولايات المتحدة الأمريكية
مؤسس ورئيس مشروع ليبيا الشفاء للدعم النفسي والاجتماعي
مستشار عيادة النفس المطمئنّة

Family Bonding Project
WORLDWIDE

www.ingramcontent.com/pod-product-compliance
Lightning Source LLC
Chambersburg PA
CBHW020618300426
44113CB00007B/686